Roe v. Wade

AND THE FIGHT OVER LIFE AND LIBERTY

by
Nancy Tompkins

Historic Supreme Court Cases
FRANKLIN WATTS
A Division of Grolier Publishing
New York London Hong Kong Sydney
Danbury, Connecticut

For my family.

Photo credits ©: AP/Wide World Photos: 95, 107, 134; Austin History Center, Austin Public Library: 19, 91, 99; Bettmann Archive: 44; Reuters/Bettmann: 120; Supreme Court of the United States: 85; UPI/Bettmann: 7, 11, 29, 31, 39, 52, 56, 59, 70, 111, 122, 124.

Library of Congress Cataloging-in-Publication Data

Tompkins, Nancy.
    Roe v. Wade: the fight over life and liberty / by Nancy Tompkins.
        p. cm. — (Historic Supreme Court cases)
    Includes bibliographical references and index.
    Summary: Examines the individuals and the issues involved in the landmark U.S. Supreme Court case that legalized abortion.
    ISBN 0-531-11286-1
    1. Roe, Jane 1947- —Trials, litigation, etc.—Juvenile literature. 2. Wade, Henry—Trials, litigation, etc. Juvenile literature. 3. Abortion—Law and legislation—United States—Juvenile literature. [1. Roe, Jane, 1947- —Trials, litigation, etc. 2. Wade, Henry—Trials, litigation, etc. 3. Trials (Abortion) 4. Abortion—Law and legislation.] I. Title. II. Series.
    KF228.R59T66 1996
    344.73'04192'0269—dc20   96-13523
    [347.30441920269]   CIP AC

CONTENTS

Chapter 1

THREE LIVES

HARRY BLACKMUN

"*Roe* against *Wade* was not such a revolutionary opinion at the time,"[1] remembers retired Supreme Court justice Harry Blackmun. His statement sounds improbable in light of the demonstrations, arson, and shootings that have marked the American debate over abortion in this decade. But history supports his impression.

Blackmun was not known for being extreme, or even liberal, at the time President Richard Nixon appointed him to the Supreme Court in 1970. The Senate had rebuffed Nixon's first two choices, both conservative southerners, after bitter confirmation fights. Finally, Nixon picked Blackmun, a Minnesotan and childhood friend of the chief justice, Warren Burger.

Blackmun had been resident legal counsel at the world famous Mayo Clinic until 1959, when he was appointed to the federal bench, and he continued to serve on the board of directors to the Rochester Methodist Hospital until Nixon tapped him to sit on the High Court. Blackmun was considered a dependably conservative Republican in the style of Burger, and the Senate confirmed his appointment unanimously. Newspapers took to calling the pair the "Minnesota Twins."

Years later, Blackmun would confess that if he had to do it all over again, he would have become a physician rather than a lawyer.[2] Short and soft-spoken, usually attired in a pale cardigan sweater, he was not by nature contentious. Most of the people who knew him, especially in his early days on the Supreme Court, were struck more by his indecision than his brilliance or passion.[3] As the years passed, he became known for working impossibly long hours and anguishing over the decisions of the Court.

Roe v. Wade was the first major opinion Justice Blackmun was assigned to write on behalf of the Court's majority, and no one would have predicted in 1973 that, for doing this task, he would be cheered and despised for decades to come. But the twenty-four years he served on the High Court saw a dramatic change in the political climate. By the time he retired in 1994, prim and unassuming Harry Blackmun, whom the comedian Garrison Keillor dubbed "the shy person's jurist," had the stature of a giant in civil rights circles. He had also inflamed a vocal segment of the American public, receiving in his career an unprecedented deluge of judicial hate mail, 60,000 letters, many laced with violent religious imagery.

His enemies called him everything from the Butcher of Dachau (Dachau was a German concentration camp during the Nazi regime) to Pontius Pilate. At a speech in 1994, he read from a letter: "'You are the lowest scum on earth'—signed by 'an American Patriot.'"[4] But they did not stop at writing. In 1984, Blackmun received death threats from an antiabortion group called the Army of God, and federal marshals were assigned to protect him. One evening a year later, as he and his wife Dorothy sat reading in the living room of their apartment in Virginia, a bullet crashed through the window, tearing a hole "the size of an orange" and spraying glass around the room.[5]

During the brief confirmation hearing that preceded his appointment, Blackmun told the Senate that he

*Justice Harry Blackmun wrote the
majority opinion in* Roe v. Wade.

would look out for the "little people" whose cases came
before the Court.[6] He had been moved, he explained,
by letters he had received since President Nixon nom-
inated him to the Court. True to his promise, and to
the profound disappointment of the president, Justice
Blackmun cast his votes over the years to protect the

rights of the powerless—the poor, the young, immigrants, and racial minorities.

In 1970, in the controversy that was to make Harry Blackmun famous, the "little people," the ones whose suffering the law had never heeded, were women. In 1965, when abortion was still prohibited in every state, illegal abortion accounted for nearly seventeen percent of all deaths related to pregnancy and childbirth. After California liberalized its laws in 1967, admissions for infection resulting from illegal abortions at Los Angeles County Medical Center fell by almost seventy-five percent. Facts like these galvanized the movement to change history that changed Harry Blackmun's life.

SARAH WEDDINGTON
Sarah Weddington is bright and plump. She dresses in good suits of peacock and fuchsia, and exudes the warmth and seamless poise of someone who was raised to be a lady. Like many Texas women of her generation, she travels with hot rollers and smiles often. Sarah Weddington lectures around the country about the constitutional right to abortion.

Born Sarah Ragle in Abilene, the daughter of a Methodist minister, Weddington grew up singing in the church choir, playing the organ, and giving Sunday devotionals. In her sophomore year at Canyon High School, she was president of the Future Homemakers of America. But inside, she strained against the limited roles she was expected to play in life. As she puts it, "We were told 'Women don't,' 'You can't,' 'That would be too strenuous for you.'"[7] She describes how women's basketball was played in West Texas when she was growing up:

Teams were composed of ten players, five on each half of the court. The players on one side of the court would work their way, two dribbles at a time, to the center of the court, where they

8

would pass the ball to teammates three inches away, who would head for the goal two dribbles at a time. I could never understand why we could not run full court, or why it was considered traveling, a technical violation, if we failed to pass the ball after two dribbles. When I persisted, I was told that running full court would be too strenuous for women. A high school physical education instructor told us, "Young women must preserve their reproductive capacity; after all, it is their meal ticket."[8]

Like most of the women at her small Methodist college, Weddington graduated with secondary-education teaching credentials. Unlike most of her classmates, however, she dreamed of becoming a lawyer. During her senior year of college, she confided her ambition to the dean. He told her not to even think of it. His *son* was in law school, he explained, and was finding it very difficult. Weddington ignored the dean's admonition and gained admission to the University of Texas School of Law.

Before she was thirty, Weddington did something only a few lawyers ever do in their careers: she argued in front of the United States Supreme Court. Her case, *Roe v. Wade*, gave American women the constitutional right to choose abortion. It is a right Weddington has been defending ever since. In 1992, at almost fifty, she wrote, "If someone had told me in 1969 that I would still be talking about abortion twenty-three years later, I would have thought that preposterous."[9] She muses about the price she has paid for her dedication to legal abortion—a ruined marriage, jobs she was never offered, children she never had. In 1992, a journalist commented that Weddington's opportunities have been "blighted by the very breakthrough that made her famous."

Sarah Weddington has also received her share of

hate mail, letters conveying messages like, "I wish your mother had aborted *you.*" She has been greeted on college campuses where she has been invited to speak by picketers bearing signs that say "Baby Killer." "Yet when people ask me if I'm tired of talking about the subject," she says, "I mean it when I say no. I care too much about the case and its future not to continue to talk."[10]

Her conviction about the abortion issue is not academic. In 1967, Sarah Ragle was in her third year of law school and working several jobs when she noticed that her period was late. She had never slept with anyone before that year, when her relationship with Ron Weddington had progressed to the point where they were talking about marriage. Ron was finishing his college degree after returning from service in the army. He planned to start law school the following summer. Sarah's mind reeled with the question: what would she do if she were pregnant? She had to keep up with her classes and jobs. Ron had years of schooling ahead, and Sarah wanted to work to support them. She confided her fears to Ron, and they discussed their options.

Abortion was illegal in Texas. Sarah knew that women in her position commonly found solutions to their problem, but she couldn't bring herself to investigate the options because she was too humiliated to tell anyone she was pregnant. Finally, Ron heard about a doctor who performed abortions south of the border. The practice was illegal in Mexico, as well as in Texas, but Ron's source told him that the doctors probably paid off the police to ignore their business.

The abortion cost Sarah's entire savings, $400—cash only. She and Ron left Austin early in the morning, checked into a motel north of the border, and then crossed into Mexico, as arranged, to meet their escort. A man appeared at the appointed place, and they followed him silently through winding dirt alleys to a small white building. Sarah was gratified

*Attorney Sarah Weddington, pictured here in
1978, sought to have a Texas statute outlawing
abortion ruled unconstitutional on behalf of her
client, a woman identified in court papers under
the assumed name of Jane Roe.*

to see that it was clean inside. When a nurse summoned her, she squeezed Ron's hand and passed through a door, as she says, to "put my life, my future, in the hands of strangers."[11]

As Weddington recounts, she was lucky. The doctor was pleasant and competent. He explained the proce-

dure to her and then instructed the nurse and anes-
thesiologist to begin. She remembers thinking before
sedation overcame her: "I hope I don't die, and I pray
that no one ever finds out about this."[12]

When she woke up, Sarah was in her motel room
bed with Ron at her side. Everything had gone
smoothly. Apart from a lingering weakness from the
anesthesia and the cramps the doctor had told her
to expect, she was fine. The next day, she and Ron
returned to their lives in Austin. And for twenty
years, Sarah Weddington kept her secret.

NORMA MCCORVEY

In 1967, the year Sarah Ragle got her Mexican abortion, Norma McCorvey was twenty years old. She had
been living on her own for years. Born Norma Nelson
in Lettesworth, Louisiana to a waitress and an army
enlisted man, McCorvey had a chaotic childhood. She
writes, "I had my first cup of coffee at age seven. I had
my first beer not long after that."[13] Her father, she
says, was kind and quiet. Her mother was beautiful
and, often, furious. One of her first memories, she
recounts, is of her mother "walking down the street,
pulling her sandal off her foot, and smacking a neighbor woman on the head, over and over."[14] Norma
never got along with her raging mother, who called
her stupid and an idiot. "When she was angry," Norma
writes, "which was just about every time she saw me,
she smacked me so hard my head hurt."[15]

When Norma was nine, her family moved to
Houston, Texas. Her parents fought almost all the
time in those days, so she tried to stay out of the
house. One day, when she came home from school, she
didn't smell the smoke from her father's cigarettes.
Her mother never would say that Norma's father had
left, but a few days later, she went to work at a depart-
ment store. She took a nighttime job, too, as a waitress
at a Houston nightclub. Even when she didn't have to

work, Norma's mother would go to the club and come home long after Norma and her brother, Jimmy, had gone to bed. When she came home and shook Norma awake, her breath always smelled of liquor.

After a year's absence, Norma's father returned, and the family moved to Dallas. Norma learned to smoke and shoplift. When she needed something for school or for Jimmy's dinner, she telephoned Lilly's Lounge, where her mother usually could be found perched on a bar stool, surrounded by men, laughing and drinking. Afternoons and weekends, Norma worked checking oil and tires and washing windshields at Don's Texaco Station. But at night, she just roamed the streets, making circles around the neighborhood. The situation at home was getting unbearable. At ten, Norma emptied the cash drawer at Don's Texaco and ran away to Oklahoma City with one of her schoolmates. For two days, the girls were very happy. Then the police came.

After a trial back in Dallas, Norma became a ward of the state of Texas. She spent what she says were the happiest years of her childhood, from age eleven to age fifteen, at the State School for Girls. Every time they released her and sent her home, she ran away again just so she would be sent back for another term. Her caseworker, Mrs. Wilson, understood what Norma was running from, but the school couldn't keep her forever. When Norma turned fifteen, Mrs. Wilson told her that she was going to be released again. But this time, she said, if Norma backslid, she would be sent to a place more like a prison than a school.

When she got back to Dallas, Norma's father had left again. Her mother was living with a man named Raymond. She told Norma that she had arranged for her to stay with a distant relative. The arrangement did not last. The relative, a big man whose name she cannot remember, came into Norma's bedroom every night and raped her. After three weeks, her mother took a good look at Norma and made her explain why she had dark circles under her eyes. When Norma told her the reason, her mother brought her to live at home.

A month with Raymond and her mother passed peacefully enough, but Norma could not stop thinking about the assaults. In search of distraction, she took a full-time job as a roller-skating waitress at a drive-in burger joint. The carhops at Cybil's dressed like cowgirls, in short, fringed skirts, buckskin vests, and cowboy hats. They packed toy pistols in leather holsters.

One afternoon, when Norma had been waitressing for a few months, a beautiful black Ford Fairlane rolled into the lot at Cybil's. The driver honked and Norma skated over. When she brought him the BLT he ordered, he asked, "What time do you get off, doll?" That was how she met Woody McCorvey, a twice-divorced, twenty-four-year-old unemployed sheet-metal worker.

Six weeks later, the two were married. Norma was sixteen. If she had had more experience, Norma might have been able to tell that marriage with Woody McCorvey was a bad bet. He had never managed to find work in Texas, and when the newlyweds descended on his parents in Pasadena, California, their reception was chilly. Most days, Woody slept until noon. Then he would climb out of bed, dress, and drive his mother around town doing errands. At night, the family argued, loudly. Most of their fights had to do with Norma: what was Woody doing with her and how long did they intend to stay?

Finally Woody found a job, and the couple moved to a tiny apartment in El Monte, California. Norma was lonely, and very soon after the move, she began to feel queasy, too. A neighbor took her to the local free clinic where the doctor confirmed that she was pregnant. Norma wasn't sure she and Woody were ready for children, but she decided to throw herself into making the best of things. She splurged on a Chef Boy-Ar-Dee spaghetti dinner, some chopped beef, and a small head of lettuce. When Woody came home, she had set the table with a red-and-white plastic cloth, a candle, and flowers from the yard stuck into an empty Coke bottle.

Norma told her husband the news. And Woody hit her, she says, "from the kitchenette clear into the living room."[16] Since neither of his other wives had conceived, he wrongly assumed that he was sterile, and that Norma had been running around. After Woody stormed out, Norma changed the locks, sold what she could of their meager possessions, and went home to Texas. Her mother took custody of Norma's daughter soon after she was born and from that moment, Norma became a drifter.

McCorvey wrote in 1992 that she has never forgiven herself for giving up her firstborn:

> *To some people, an eighteen-year-old . . . waitress might not have seemed like a good mother for a baby. But these people never knew the love I had, and still have, for [my daughter]. In my mind and in my heart, I know I would have been a good mother to her. And our lives—both of our lives—would have turned out completely differently.*
>
> *It was a possibility worth dying for. But I didn't. Not then, anyway. Instead, I failed my daughter. At the moment she needed me I failed her totally. I've lived to blame myself for my failure ever since. And I will take that sorrow to my grave.[17]*

Norma had long felt that she was lesbian, and she settled into a series of relationships with different women. She continued to have occasional affairs with men, though, and every time she did, she got pregnant. She had another baby in 1969, which she gave over to its father, a man she identifies only as "Joe."

The year 1970 found Norma McCorvey in Florida,

working as a barker with a traveling carnival. The discovery that she was pregnant for the third time plunged her into a pit of despair. She writes, "I was a deadbeat, a bum, a twenty-one-year-old nobody at the end of my rope."[18] She was broke. And she was worn out. She knew she would have to stop working as soon as her condition began to show. A friend wired her bus fare to Dallas, and Norma rode home, carrying what she now calls "the *Roe* baby" inside her.

Twenty-five years later, Norma McCorvey would be baptized in a public swimming pool with flash bulbs popping and reporters scurrying around the perimeter. She would appear on television to tell the country she had found Jesus Christ and decided abortion was wrong. But in 1970, riding the Greyhound bus from Jacksonville to Dallas, Norma McCorvey was just a poor lost soul, wishing desperately for "a way to get unpregnant."[19]

Chapter 2

STIRRINGS IN AUSTIN

Austin is the seat of government in what most Texans are pleased to say is a big and steadfastly conservative state. But the city hums with progressive talk. Austin's unique character among Texas towns is due, in part, to the institution that sits at its heart. The University of Texas (UT) campus begins just five blocks north of the state capitol. Both research-oriented and well endowed, UT draws an impressive array of scholars from around the world into the city to study and teach. Beside its natural beauty, Austin's great charm is that, amid the broad and diverse social climate engendered by the university, it still feels like Texas. It is a down-to-earth city where people can go almost anywhere in cowboy boots.

In 1967, Austin was different in many ways from the West Texas towns where Sarah Weddington had grown up. But it was not entirely different. Sex discrimination was still alive and well. Although Sarah graduated that year in the top quarter of her law school class, no law firm offered her a job. She was relieved and grateful when one of her professors, John Sutton, asked her to work as his assistant on a multi-year project, and she settled into a little office in the building that housed the UT law library.

Sarah had always known that she wanted to do more with her life than Texas ladies were encouraged to do, but she had never identified her yearning with any larger social movement. She had not become involved in the campus politics that marked the 1960s, in part, because she had been too busy. Throughout law school, she had held down one job or another—as a secretary, insurance clerk, hospital librarian, and sorority house mother—to support herself. But even more so, she had resisted social activism because, despite her unusual ambition, Sarah was resolutely proper; her church-centered upbringing had left her fundamentally unsuited to be part of the counterculture. One close acquaintance at the time later said that Sarah's manner and outlook had made her seem "more like my parents than like a peer." Sarah herself explains, "I had never even been to a party where liquor was served until after I graduated from college."[1]

In March 1969, the nation was coming apart at the seams. Riots had wasted cities, and violent protests had broken out on university campuses. Martin Luther King, Jr., and Robert F. Kennedy had been assassinated, and Richard Nixon had won the presidency by promising "a return to law and order."[2] A handful of smart and independent women had converged and found each other at the University of Texas.

Judy Smith, a native of Oklahoma with a chemistry degree from Brandeis, had spent a year in West Africa with the Peace Corps before she came to Austin to get her Ph.D. in molecular biology. She was accepted at UT in spite of an undergraduate professor who refused to write a recommendation for her, although she had received one of two A's in his class, because he didn't believe in giving recommendations to women.[3] Victoria "Vic" Foe was another biology student, and Barbara Hines was a graduate student in Latin American studies. Beatrice Vogel had two small children and a doctorate in biology from Yale.

The world of Austin student activism revolved around the *Rag*, a two-year-old underground newspa-

*An aerial view of Austin, Texas, in 1966.
The impetus for* Roe v. Wade *originated in Austin
within a group of University of Texas students
who operated a pregnancy and reproduction
counseling service.*

per published by a loose organization of former and current UT students. The paper publicized happenings in the city and around the country. It advised on such things as "when the free health care clinic would be open, what to do if a person was arrested in a protest, where to find the best music in town, and when the next meeting of student and activist organizations would be."[4] Many *Rag* writers also belonged to the local chapter of Students for a Democratic Society (SDS), a national organization of college and graduate students who are active in advancing a variety of progressive social causes. At the newspaper, Judy Smith met Jim Wheelis, a law school classmate of Ron Weddington. Through her graduate work and SDS, she met Vic, Barbara, and Bea.

The SDS's National Council met in Austin in March 1969, and the sexist behavior of the group's male leaders left members of the local chapter surprised and disgusted. The council's visit crystallized a feeling among the Austin women that the social revolution they had worked to bring about had overlooked them. After some discussion, they resolved to work on their own cause. In the spring, a group of eight or ten began meeting once a week to talk about gender and women's roles.

Their discussions frequently focused on contraception and abortion. They talked about how women could not truly direct their own lives, control their physical and psychological health, or make education and career plans if they could not control the number and frequency of their pregnancies. The *Rag* began to reflect these conversations. In April 1969, a brief story appeared describing how Austin women seeking abortions could drive south into Mexico, where doctors provided safe services for less than four hundred dollars.[5]

The University Board of Regents had always been nervous about the *Rag*'s incendiary influence over the student population and, in the summer of 1969, the university administration banned the sale of the newspaper on campus. The *Rag*'s staff was outraged. They considered the university's action to be a violation of the First Amendment freedom of the press, and they persuaded a local attorney to sue the Board of Regents on their behalf in federal court. The presses continued to roll, and the *Rag* continued to circulate off-campus while the staff awaited the court's decision.

Meanwhile, the women's group continued to meet. In July 1969, Judy Smith published an essay in the *Rag* reflecting the group's thoughts. "We in Women's Liberation," she wrote, "deny any inherent differences between men and women and regard everyone as human beings with the same potential. . . . We are questioning the ideals of marriage and motherhood" and the "society that has created these roles and values."[6]

The Austin women were not alone. Women throughout the nation were challenging the ideal of motherhood as every woman's primary destiny. The fact that abortion carried criminal penalties in every state of the union did not transform every woman who became pregnant into a woman who was satisfied with her condition. What it did was to create a booming underground market in the termination of pregnancy. "By the late 1960s as many as 1,200,000 women were undergoing illegal abortions each year: more than one criminal abortion a minute."[7] In 1970, the Nixon Report on Crime listed illegal abortions as the third most lucrative enterprise of organized crime.[8]

Women who could afford the trip ended their pregnancies in other countries where abortion was legal or where it was illegal but dependably underprosecuted. An American Airlines flight attendant based in Dallas in the 1960s noticed that the Friday-morning flight to El Paso, Texas, was almost always booked solid with women. When she commented on this observation to an older attendant, she was told that that was the "abortion flight." As many as twenty women on any given Friday were flying to El Paso to cross the border into Mexico for an abortion.[9] As a handful of states liberalized their laws, travel between states for the purpose of obtaining legal abortions became so common that the practice acquired a name: "abortion tourism."[10]

Women without the money to travel tried home remedies to end their unwanted pregnancies. The *Rag* printed public service articles cautioning women about unsafe abortion methods: the dangers of drinking poison, inserting knitting needles, paintbrushes, telephone wire, curtain rods, ballpoint pens, chopsticks, and coat hangers, or introducing alcohol, soapsuds, lye, and Lysol, into the uterus. Most such methods usually failed to cause an abortion, the articles warned, but often led to permanent disability, infection, or death for the woman.[11]

By the end of the summer of 1969, the Austin women's discussion group had decided they were ready to do more. They had talked since the spring about how difficult it could be for unmarried UT students to get contraceptives or even birth control counseling. Some physicians simply refused such requests from women who did not have husbands, and the local Planned Parenthood clinic did not serve UT students. In early September, the discussion group announced its plan to fill this void by establishing a resource room for contraceptive information. A month later, the Women's Liberation Birth Control Information Center opened in a tiny cubicle next to the *Rag*'s office in the university YMCA. Every weekday, from 3:00 P.M. to 8:00 P.M., one or more volunteers from the discussion group staffed the office.[12]

Although the group had not intended the birth control project to address questions about abortion, it soon became apparent that the issue would be unavoidable. Everybody knew that abortion was illegal in Texas, yet every day, the Women's Liberation volunteers fielded at least a half dozen face-to-face inquiries from women seeking to terminate their pregnancies. They began quietly to seek out dependable information about the availability of safe abortions that they could pass on to the women who sought their help.[13]

Nationally, a vast network of clergymen from different faiths was doing the same thing. In May 1967, twenty-one Protestant ministers and Jewish rabbis had made a stunning announcement, reported on the front page of the *New York Times*, offering to refer women to doctors who were performing safe abortions. Their organization, the Clergy Consultation Service on Abortion, drew thousands of "gentle lawbreakers" into the fray.[14] The group announced its credo:

> *A belief in the "sanctity of human life" certainly includes helpfulness and sympathy to the women forced by the present law into criminality. We are mindful that there are doctors who in their wisdom perform therapeutic abortions outside the present legal restrictions. When a physician performs such an operation, motivated by compassion and concern for the patient and not simply for monetary gain, we do not regard him as a criminal but living by the highest standard of the Hippocratic oath. . . . Therefore, to that end we are establishing a Pregnancy Consultation service, including referral to the best available medical advice and aid to the women in need.*

Members of the Clergy Consultation Service followed strict procedures. They interviewed practitioners, ascertained their prices, and inspected their facilities. They collected follow-up data from women they counseled about how they had been treated. After a cooperating pastor or rabbi counseled a pregnant woman who then decided to end her pregnancy, the clergyman would recommend places she might go to for a safe abortion, either legal or illegal. Their highest goal was to protect the woman's health.[15]

The Austin chapter of the Clergy Consultation Service and the volunteers at the UT project agreed to work together so that more clinics could be inspected and more women served. To keep them from falling into the hands of police or incompetent abortionists, "women having abortions were given very specific instructions. They were told where to park their cars, where the building was and what it would look like, where the office was and what the doctor should look like. Passwords and code words were used to ensure that the women were treated only by the prearranged doctors."[16]

Of course, advertising abortion referral services was out of the question. Most of the women involved with the UT project had had or at least witnessed their share of run-ins between students and police during the tumultuous sixties. The Texas abortion statute not only made it illegal for a person to perform an abortion; it also made it a crime to give a woman "the means for procuring an abortion." Anyone convicted under either provision could be sent to prison for two to five years. The volunteers wondered: could telling a woman where she could get an abortion be interpreted as giving her "the means" to procure an abortion? Could they be jailed for what they were doing?

Many *Rag* staffers and other student activists already worried that they were being watched by the police. Their fears were not unfounded. Years later, Barbara Hines petitioned under the federal Freedom of Information Act to obtain a copy of her FBI record. It read in part: "Barbara Hines has been involved with Women's Liberation and interested in Women's Abortion Action Coalition. . . . [According to sources,] Women's Liberation is basically opposed to male chauvinism to the point of eliminating the wearing of brassieres and clean attire in order not to be a sex symbol. The group also favors abortions."[17]

Despite the need for secrecy, word of mouth had brought women out of the woodwork seeking the referral project's services. Some volunteers were beginning to feel the pressure of operating a high-volume covert enterprise, but, because of the possible legal risks, it was not easy to find others willing to take over. At the same time, members of the group were concerned that the project was not reaching the vast majority of women who wanted to end their pregnancies. They hated to think of women landing in hospital emergency rooms or worse when reliable counsel was free and available right in Austin. They decided to seek the advice of a lawyer.

In November 1969, Sarah Weddington was well into her second year of work for John Sutton. She had stayed largely on the sidelines of political activism at UT, although her husband, Ron, was a close friend and law school classmate of Judy Smith's friend, Jim Wheelis, and had even lent his name to the *Rag*'s lawsuit against the UT regents. Sarah's style was different; she seemed more "proper" than the women who launched and staffed the abortion referral project, but because of her secret trip to Mexico, her convictions ran deeper than others might have guessed. Weddington says: "*Roe v. Wade* started at a garage sale."[18]

It was a sparkling Saturday morning. Sarah, Judy Smith, and Bea Vogel were sorting through second-hand clothes, arranging them on a big folding table for sale. The Weddingtons' garage had become the site for many of their friends' political fundraising efforts. Judy, a deep thinker, was more talkative than usual that Saturday. She told Sarah she wanted the referral project to be able to offer its services openly, but she confided her worries about the legal consequences. Would the public provision of abortion information leave the project's volunteers vulnerable to arrest and prosecution? Sarah didn't know, but she agreed to do some research.

What exactly did the Texas antiabortion law mean? The question seemed simple enough. Weddington settled into the UT law library with the statute book. The legislature had passed the law in 1854. The main provision made it illegal for anyone to perform an abortion or to give a woman something that would cause her to abort. The penalty for violating that provision was two to five years in prison. If the woman had not consented, the penalty was double. The provision that worried the Women's Liberation group said that anyone who "furnished the means for procuring an abortion" was guilty as an accomplice. Other provisions said that the fine for attempting to perform an abortion—even if the attempt failed—was $100 to $1,000; and that if a woman died because of an abortion or attempted abortion, her death would be prosecuted as murder. The only legal abortion in Texas was one "procured or attempted by medical advice for the purpose of saving the life" of the woman.[19]

Weddington knew that courts were not in the business of second-guessing the wisdom of properly enacted laws. It would not matter in court, for example, if she could prove that every woman the group helped had sought their services voluntarily, terminated her pregnancy with no ill effects on her health, and lived her life happily ever afterward. She knew that if any of her friends was brought up on criminal charges, there would be only two questions: one legal, for the judge, and one factual, for the jury. The judge would have to decide what the legislature had in mind when it wrote the Texas law. Had it intended to criminalize abortion *referral* when it prohibited "furnishing the means" to procure an abortion? If the judge answered that question in the affirmative, then it would be for the jury to determine whether volunteers in the Austin group had, in fact, referred women to abortion providers.

Because there was no doubt that her friends were doing exactly that, Weddington focused on the legal question: was giving information "furnishing the means" to procure an abortion? The handful of Texas cases she found that interpreted the statute shed little light. A few doctors had been prosecuted for performing abortions. There was no case addressing the murkier issue of abortion referral. She turned her attention to the legislative history: why had the state legislature prohibited abortion to begin with? The answer to that question, at least, was clear, if surprising. The earliest laws against abortion had nothing to do with fetuses' rights. They were concerned with women's health.

Abortion, it turned out, had not been at all unusual in the United States during the late eighteenth and early nineteenth centuries. But the primitive methods commonly prescribed to end a pregnancy in the 1800s were as dangerous as those the *Rag* had warned against in 1969. In the nineteenth century, it was popular, for example, to administer poisons to pregnant women to induce abortion (on the dubious theory that the right dose would be enough to kill the fetus but too little to kill the woman). Mortality from surgical abortions was also extremely high at the time, because science had not yet discovered antibiotics to prevent infection. Statistics from New York in the early nineteenth century showed a thirty percent death rate from infections after surgical abortion, even when performed in hospitals![20] Against this backdrop, the state's early interest in regulating abortion was not just understandable; it was compelling.

Of course, by 1969, the concerns that had originally animated abortion laws were obsolete. In the 115 years since Texas had outlawed abortion, medical science had advanced to the point that surgical abortion was safer than childbirth. But over the same period, new ideas about fetal rights, strongly held and widely propagated by the Roman Catholic church, had

27

ascended to justify the old laws, and the laws had never been repealed. Weddington found it ironic that prohibitions meant in the beginning to preserve women's health were now the greatest obstacles preventing them from getting competent care. Abortion, properly done, could be virtually painless and perfectly safe. But the law drove women underground, where they faced nineteenth-century risks: excruciating pain, infection, disability, and even death. Weddington reported the inconclusive results of her research to Judy Smith, and the referral project's efforts continued in secrecy as before.

Toward the end of November, a three-judge panel assembled in Austin to hear oral arguments in the *Rag*'s federal case against the UT Board of Regents. The community of student activists buzzed with excitement over the newspaper's having invoked such a formal and impressive display by asserting their First Amendment rights against the board. Judy Smith, still mulling over her worries about the referral project, wondered if the federal courts might be receptive to a similar constitutional challenge to the Texas abortion law. Over breakfast, she asked her friend, Jim Wheelis, what it would take to sue the state. Jim shrugged and said, "About fifteen dollars and an attorney."[21]

By afternoon, Judy Smith had broached the subject with the only likely attorney she knew. Sarah Weddington was more than a little surprised at the suggestion that *she* should file a lawsuit in federal court. She explained to Judy, "You need someone older and with more experience. You need somebody in a [law] firm, with research and secretarial backup."[22] She said she would think about it.

A few days later, when Weddington was in Dallas, she remembered Linda Coffee, one of the other four women who, along with 120 men, had entered UT law school with Sarah in the summer of 1965. Like Sarah, Linda had always been a strong student. After graduat-

*In May 1944, police carry a woman out of a
Brooklyn, New York, apartment after she underwent
an illegal abortion. Police had raided the apartment
after receiving information that a doctor was
performing abortions there.*

ing, she had taken a prestigious yearlong clerkship in Dallas with the Honorable Sarah T. Hughes, a federal judge, and when she took the Texas bar exam in the spring of 1968, she tied for the second-highest score in the state. By the end of 1969, Coffee was working at Palmer & Palmer, a small bankruptcy firm in Dallas.

Weddington called Coffee on December 3 to ask if she would consider filing a federal case challenging the Texas abortion statute. She explained the situation of her friends in Austin and said that her idea was to bring the suit on their behalf. Coffee was enthusiastic at the prospect of asserting a constitutional right to abortion in the federal courts, but she doubted whether the Austin group had legal standing to challenge the law.

Her concern was that the Constitution gives federal courts only limited authority, or jurisdiction, to hear claims litigants wish to make. The principal restriction on the courts' power, known as the case-or-controversy requirement, demands that people who want relief from the federal courts have an actual dispute that they *personally* need resolved. The standing doctrine prevents anyone from raising another person's legal rights. As the Supreme Court has explained, to be heard in federal court, "[a] plaintiff must allege personal injury [that is] fairly traceable to the defendant's allegedly unlawful conduct and likely to be redressed by the requested relief."[23]

Coffee felt certain that a pregnant woman who wanted an abortion, because of her intensely personal interest in the matter, would have standing to sue Texas to undo the law. She was not so sure that the Austin Women's Liberation volunteers acquired such a stake simply by encouraging and advising other people who wished to violate the Texas abortion statute.

With these doubts, Coffee and Weddington agreed that it would be best to assemble a group of plaintiffs,

*Attorney Linda Coffee, pictured here in 1972,
joined Sarah Weddington in challenging
Texas's antiabortion law.*

each with a different interest in the case. That way, if
the court decided that one claimant's interest was not
sufficiently personal or compelling to confer standing,
it could dismiss that claimant without dismissing the
entire lawsuit.

They found a married couple, David and Marsha
King, who were passionately interested in challenging

31

the Texas abortion law. Marsha had become pregnant after she switched from birth control pills to a diaphragm on the advice of a doctor whom she had consulted to treat a strange onset of vision problems, severe backaches, and alarming mood swings. The Kings were not ready to parent a child, and the pregnancy, in combination with the medications Marsha was taking for her back pain and depression, made her so sick that she could barely work. Marsha had flown to Mexico City and undergone a lengthy and painful abortion. On the plane back to Dallas, she was relieved and happy, but so weak that the flight attendants had to give her oxygen. The experience left her and David outraged, and firmly convinced that the state had no business interfering with a woman's desire to end her pregnancy.

Even with the Kings signed on, Weddington and Coffee worried that a federal court would dismiss the case. The Kings plainly had *once* had a "controversy" with the state. But a court might say that the controversy had evaporated with Marsha's Mexican abortion. Because Marsha King could no longer complain that Texas was preventing her from having an abortion, the court might conclude that the "case or controversy" was over, and that her claim was moot. The attorneys decided they needed a *pregnant* woman who would continue her pregnancy despite her wish to end it, though, as Coffee later said, "I didn't know how we would find" such a woman.[24]

Chapter 3

ENTER JANE ROE

Norma McCorvey had returned to Dallas flat broke, pregnant, and so tired and low that she spent her first five days in town wandering around inside the Dallas bus station. Finally, she placed a telephone call to the Rendezvous, a lesbian club where she use to tend bar. Everyone at the club knew her as Pixie. Roz, an old friend, took her in hand. Within a week, Norma had a job and an apartment. It felt almost like old times. Except that she couldn't really convince herself that everything was the same. She couldn't stand to think of the baby she was carrying. She didn't want to give birth, she didn't want the child, and she didn't want to go through giving it up.

McCorvey was pouring out her woes one night as she worked. From across the bar, a customer said, "you don't want to have this baby? Why don't you get rid of it?"[1] Norma had no idea what she was talking about. She walked away from the customer and grabbed her friend Jinx by the arm. "Can you believe what that girl over there told me?" she whispered. "She said I didn't have to be pregnant anymore. She said if I didn't want to have a baby, I could just get rid of it!" Jinx looked at her, puzzled, and then her face softened. "Oh, Pixie," she said, "didn't you know that doctors can stop a woman from being pregnant?"[2]

For the rest of the night, Norma was so happy, she felt dizzy. First thing the next morning, she called the obstetrician who had delivered her first two babies and made an appointment. For three days, waiting to see Dr. Brady, she walked on air, knowing that she was going to be delivered from her predicament. Finally in his office, she explained what she wanted. He looked at her frowning, and spoke slowly. "Norma, I don't do abortions. And I don't know anyone who does. In fact, if I heard of anyone who was doing them, I'd have to report them to the AMA."[3] Norma was stunned as he explained that abortion was illegal in Texas. Utterly deflated, she let Dr. Brady give her the phone number of an attorney who handled adoptions.

Two weeks later, she was in the law offices of Henry McCluskey, telling him how she had already given up two children, telling him how desperately she wished she weren't pregnant. McCluskey listened with concern. "Norma," he said gently, "you know that abortions are illegal in Texas, don't you?"[4]

McCorvey said she didn't care. "Can't you put me in touch with a doctor who does them anyway?"[5] she asked.

At that, McCluskey shook his head. "Absolutely not," he said sadly. He listened while Norma poured out her frustration and despair. Finally he said, "Do you feel that strongly about getting an abortion?"[6]

Norma looked at him evenly and nodded. She told him she would get an abortion with or without his help. Wherever she could find one.[7]

Then McCluskey got agitated. He warned her that illegal abortion was dangerous, and often fatal. Finally, he seemed to come to a decision. He told Norma about two young lawyers he knew who were looking for a pregnant woman who wanted an abortion. "A woman just like you," he said. "The reason is, they need her to add her name to a lawsuit, to help them overturn the Texas law against abortions."

"Will it help me get an abortion?" she asked.

"To be honest with you, Norma," he said, "I don't know."[8]

She agreed to let him give her name to Sarah Weddington and Linda Coffee.

The three women met a few weeks later at a pizza parlor in Dallas. They made an odd trio. Coffee was dark and lean, and Weddington, blond and plump. Both wore business suits. McCorvey, petite with an upturned nose, wore jeans and sandals and a button-down shirt tied at the waist. A bandanna around her left leg signified that she didn't have a girlfriend. It was obvious to Norma even before she sat down that Sarah and Linda didn't know any people like her.[9] The three struggled to make small talk.

While McCorvey waited at the counter to order, she gathered the courage to ask the only thing she wanted to know. She returned to the table with a pitcher of beer.

"Do you know where I can get an abortion?" she asked.

"No," said Weddington, "I don't."[10]

But instead of launching into a discussion of adoption, as Dr. Brady and Henry McCluskey had done, Sarah began asking Norma questions.

"Do you really want an abortion?" she asked. And, "why?"

McCorvey explained that she couldn't find work when she was pregnant, and that, without working, she couldn't take care of herself, much less anyone else.

"Norma," Sarah said, "do you know what the abortion process is? Do you know what women have to go through when they get one?"[11]

McCorvey had to admit that she didn't. Sarah described the procedure, which sounded awful, but not far different from what Norma had imagined. Finally, Sarah leaned forward.

"Norma. Don't you think women should have access to abortions? Safe, legal abortions?"[12]

Norma readily agreed. "But there aren't any legal ones around," she pointed out. "So I guess I've got to find an illegal one, don't I?"

Both Sarah and Linda spoke together, "No!"

At this point McCorvey was piqued. She knew that women had abortions, and she was determined to find one. "Why the hell not?" she asked.

"Because they're dangerous, Norma," said Sarah. "Illegal abortions are dangerous."

"Yeah, so?" Norma asked.[13] It was a risk she was willing to take.

And then, as McCorvey remembers, Weddington began to tell her "horror stories" of women who had had illegal abortions and lived to regret them; of others who hadn't survived the dangerous ministrations of gangsters or shady doctors, women "who'd gone home and bled to death."[14] Such horror stories are well documented, although McCorvey may exaggerate the lengths to which Weddington went that night in the pizza parlor to discourage her from seeking an illegal abortion.

Hearing the stories, McCorvey recounts, made her cry. She accepted consolation and a tissue from Weddington, who said, "I know. It really is unfair. And no one should have to go through it. Rich or poor. Anywhere." That's why, she explained, she and Coffee were working to overturn the Texas abortion law in court. Weddington said it would not be an easy thing to do. It would take a lot of work, plus a pregnant woman like McCorvey, who wanted but wasn't able to get an abortion, to put her name on the lawsuit. But if they succeeded, she said, then abortion would be legal in the state of Texas.[15]

When she heard this, McCorvey was flooded with new hope. With some hesitation, she told the attorneys about her life and her struggles, the two children she had already given up. She didn't know how they would react. She was fairly certain neither Weddington nor Coffee had "gone to reform school or dealt drugs or been beaten by their husbands or spent their days and nights in gay bars."[16] She could see the doubt and worry on their faces as she talked. She imagined the questions going through their minds: How could this woman who says she's a lesbian have gotten herself pregnant all these times? Is she lying? Maybe there's something we don't understand about her. Something weird. Something dangerous. Something that will hurt our lawsuit.[17]

Finally, Coffee and Weddington looked at each other. McCorvey could see that they had resolved to go forward. "Well, anyway, we would like to have you as a plaintiff in our lawsuit. Would you like to help us?" Weddington asked.

"Yeah," McCorvey said, trying to sound cool. But she wondered, a plaintiff? What is that? Well, she'd look it up in the dictionary later. The important thing was she hadn't lost this chance.[18]

The three women drank a toast to the lawsuit. Weddington and Coffee told McCorvey she would have to sign some papers, under a pseudonym if she preferred. They would be in touch.

When McCorvey went to Coffee's office a few weeks later to sign her statement, Coffee's secretary "commented that she looked like a small woman carrying a *big* watermelon."

On March 3, 1970, Coffee filed two lawsuits in the Dallas district court. One described the Kings, who were given the names John and Mary Doe in court papers, and the problems the Texas abortion law posed for them in light of Marsha's health conditions. The suit alleged that, given the unavailability of safe abortion, the fear of an unintended pregnancy was "having a detrimental effect upon [the Does'] marital happiness."[20] To raise the question of the legality of abortion referral services, the suit also mentioned that Mary Doe feared prosecution for having told some women where they could find abortion services south of the border.

The second suit described the predicament of Norma McCorvey, under the name Jane Roe. The Texas law, it said, infringed upon *Roe*'s "right to safe and adequate medical advice pertaining to the decision of whether to carry a given pregnancy to term" and upon "the fundamental right of all women to choose whether to bear children." It also alleged that the statute infringed upon *Roe*'s "right to privacy in the physician-patient relationship," and upon her "right to life" as protected by the Fourteenth Amendment.[21]

Both suits named as the defendant Dallas County District Attorney Henry Wade. Wade was the official responsible for the arrest and prosecution of people in the county who violated the Texas law. The suits requested the court to declare the Texas law unconstitutional and to tell Wade to stop enforcing it.

In August 1985, the *Dallas Morning News* described Henry Wade like this: "Henry Wade drawls. He drops the ending from words and says 'cain't' for 'can't.' He chews cigars and spits tobacco juice. He plays a tough game of dominoes and prefers not to travel further than Forney. Pop the ruddy face, white hair, and bulging waistline of the Dallas district attorney into a seersucker suit, and it's easy to picture him shuffling around a sleepy county courthouse."[22]

But Weddington and Coffee had no illusions about what they were up against. Henry Wade was no buffoon. In the twenty years since he had first been elected to the local prosecutor's post, the DA had earned a reputation for fair-minded toughness; years later people who had watched Wade's career remembered that he had successfully prosecuted and jailed one of his own brothers for drunk driving.[23] He had

Dallas County District Attorney Henry Wade
was named as the defendant in the two lawsuits that
Weddington and Coffee filed challenging the
constitutionality of the Texas antiabortion law.

also convicted Jack Ruby for killing President Kennedy's assassin, Lee Harvey Oswald. By the end of his thirty-five-year career as a DA, Henry Wade had sent twenty-nine people to death row.[24]

Although abortion was illegal in Texas, neither Wade's office nor the Dallas police had shown particular zeal in going after abortionists. Most of the prosecutions Wade oversaw were of unskilled practitioners who had badly or fatally injured one or more women. "Wade himself, . . . supervising a staff of more than 100 attorneys and with no particular interest in the subject matter, made no effort to have any direct input into his office's response to the two abortion cases in which he had been named the sole . . . defendant."[25]

Chapter 4
A CONSTITUTIONAL CLAIM

There were two driving forces behind *Roe v. Wade*: fear and a sense of injustice. People were violating the Texas abortion law. They were afraid of being arrested because they knew that if a trial were held, the evidence would show they were guilty. They *had* broken the law. Yet they strongly believed that guilt or innocence was beside the point. They believed *the law itself* was wrong.

This was the claim Sarah Weddington and Linda Coffee made by filing a constitutional challenge to the Texas abortion statute. Their argument bypassed questions of guilt or innocence altogether. They conceded that their plaintiffs were guilty—that they had broken, or wanted to break, the Texas law. (In fact, the "guilt" of the plaintiffs was a prerequisite to filing the lawsuit; "guilt" was necessary to show that they had standing to sue the state.) But then they invoked a higher law than the one passed by the Texas legislature: the United States Constitution. Our plaintiffs may have broken the Texas law, Weddington and Coffee asserted, but by criminalizing abortion, *the state of Texas* had broken the higher law.

The Constitution, the higher law, is what saves the United States from the tyranny of absolute democracy. Democracy means "government by the people." In a pure democracy, in the style of ancient Athens, for example, the majority would rule, plain

41

ROE v. WADE

and simple. There, the basic directive "one person, one vote" would enable a large number of men to subjugate a smaller number of women; a large number of Presbyterians to extract devotion to Jesus Christ from a smaller number of Muslims; or a large number of patriots to prevent a smaller number of anarchists from even talking about revolution.

The United States, however, is a "constitutional democracy." This description conveys the idea very accurately: the Constitution *qualifies* our democracy. Here, as in a pure democracy, the majority decides most things. Majority-elected representatives, such as the members of Congress or of the Texas legislature, write the majority's values into law. The law, then, prohibits doing things that most people agree should not be done, such as murder, theft, drug trafficking, or jaywalking. Legislators are generally free to propose and enact any law they like, however silly, shortsighted, or mean-spirited. The assumption is that they won't stray too far from the agenda of the majority who elected them because if they do, the same majority will vote them out of office the next time around.

In a *constitutional* democracy like ours, however, there are some laws legislators may not enact, even if a majority of their constituents want them to. This restraint comes from the Constitution, the higher law, which announces certain values—equality, dignity, and freedom—that no majority may override. Courts interpret these constitutional values to encircle certain rights with "law-free" zones. It is because gender equality, freedom of belief, and freedom of expression are now recognized as constitutional values that, in America, a majority cannot enact laws intended to subjugate women, coerce devotion, or silence speech. The Constitution, then, is an *antimajoritarian* instrument. It trumps the will of the majority, saving us from our own occasional intolerance and ensuring individuals the autonomy to make certain important choices even in troubled and confusing times.

Since 1803, when the Supreme Court settled the question, no one has disputed that the Constitution is the "supreme law of the land," higher than any legislative pronouncement, state or federal. Everyone agrees that when a state or federal law conflicts with the Constitution, the law must be struck down. Whether a conflict *exists,* however, is usually an open question because what the Constitution means is not self-evident.

It is not obvious, for example, that the "freedom of speech" protected by the First Amendment encompasses the freedom to dance on stage for money wearing a G-string and pasties, but in a 1991 case, the Supreme Court accepted this proposition with little debate.[1] What is obvious is that the men who wrote the First Amendment never dreamed that it would safeguard the professional expression of erotic dancers working in adult theatres. But neither did that certainty sway the Supreme Court's 1991 decision. It is widely understood that the men who wrote the Constitution in the late eighteenth century undertook to steer us through a future they could not imagine. They hoped *not* to tether the nation to their own time-bound vision. In fact, James Madison, one of the chief architects of the Constitution, insisted that his notes from the Constitutional Convention not be published until after his death. Madison wrote, "As a guide in expounding and applying the provisions of the Constitution, the debates and incidental decisions of the Convention can have no authoritative character." Madison worried that his personal knowledge of the views expressed by delegates to the Constitutional Convention were a source of "bias" in his own interpretation of the Constitution.[2]

The spacious language of our national charter

*Delegates at the Constitution Convention await
their turn to sign the U.S. Constitution.
The Constitution provides citizens with certain
rights that no law may override.*

poses a dilemma for anyone trying to figure out exactly what rights it protects. On the one hand, the Constitution doesn't spell out everything in fine print. That means that when a lawsuit requires a determination of what a particular provision of the Constitution means, judges have to bring something of themselves—reasoned judgment, a knowledge of law and history, as well as a sense for deeply rooted American values—to the task of interpretation. On the other hand, they are not supposed to bring *too much* of themselves to the job. Judges, no less than everyone else, no less than James Madison in 1791, are time-bound, helplessly shortsighted. But as guardians of the Constitution, they have a special responsibility to avoid enshrining their own moral vision in the document meant to steer the nation through a distant and uncharted future. As noted lawyer and future Supreme Court justice Louis Brandeis wrote in 1908, it is the great virtue "of a written constitution that it . . . gives a permanence and stability to popular government which otherwise would be lacking."[3]

Judges have other reasons as well to show restraint in interpreting the Constitution. Every time a court discovers or broadens a constitutional right, it inhibits democracy—and, presumably, frustrates a majority—by expanding a "law-free" zone. Carrying on this business with no armies to enforce their pronouncements, courts have a very high stake in maintaining their own credibility. The words inscribed in the Constitution are the sole source of courts' authority, and if the courts cannot explain how those words justify their pronouncements, they place their legitimacy in question.

Lower courts, state and federal, have the power to say what the Constitution means, but their interpretations can be appealed up through a chain of more powerful courts to the United States Supreme Court, the "court of last resort." Once the Supreme Court has had its say, there can be no further appeals, *and* no further debate in the lower courts about the meaning of the disputed constitutional language. The U.S. Supreme Court has the last word.

Although the meaning of the Constitution is the subject of constant and furious debate, the process of interpreting the document must proceed slowly and deliberately. Courts may not simply publish tracts describing the dimensions of constitutional rights in the name of settling hypothetical disputes and sparing would-be litigants time and trouble. The case-or-controversy requirement demands that they answer only active constitutional questions, only one at a time, and only upon the request of litigants who are embroiled in a genuine conflict.

So the revelation of constitutional rights proceeds ritually: A legislature passes a law that offends, say, an erotic dancer who has legal standing to challenge the law in court. The dancer files a lawsuit invoking the higher law. She asserts that the legislature's enactment conflicts with one or more specific provisions of the Constitution. The official charged with defending the law files a response asserting that there is no conflict. The Court determines who is correct and, incidentally, reveals something about the size and shape of the constitutional guarantee or guarantees the dancer has invoked. The idea is that our basic rights are always there embedded in the document, but the courts are not free to discover and announce them until they are infringed *and* the infringement is challenged.

The claimant in this ritual asserts that there is a previously unrecognized right in the Constitution, and asks the Court to acknowledge it. The claimant will typically suggest as many strongholds for the right as she can find in the words of the Constitution. In this way, she can "argue in the alternative," urging the Court to look for the right in one place if it is not to be found in another. New strongholds suggest themselves over time as lawyers mull over the text of the Constitution and as the Supreme Court sheds new light on its meaning by deciding new cases.

The attorneys in *Roe*, for example, argued that a woman's right to end her pregnancy could be found in the implied constitutional right to privacy, in the First Amendment's guarantee of religious freedom, and in the Fourteenth Amendment's promise to women of "equal protection" of the laws. More recently, legal scholars have also argued that the right to abortion can be found in the Thirteenth Amendment's prohibition of slavery.

Although many of these claims, at first blush, sound far-fetched, remember that the Supreme Court has been expounding the meaning of the Constitution for more than two hundred years. Anyone seeking to discover what, say, the First Amendment means must examine not only the forty-five words of that Amendment, but also the hundreds of opinions the Supreme Court has written about it as well. In essence, the Constitution expresses the general idea, and the Court supplies the fine print. It is the Court's unfolding of the First Amendment that brought us from freedom of speech in 1791 to our understanding in 1991 of erotic dancing as a kind of statement that free people should be permitted to make or "hear."

President Woodrow Wilson wrote of this process: "As the life of the nation changes so must the interpretation of the document which contains it change, by a nice adjustment, determined, not by the original intention of those who drew the paper, but by the exigencies and the new aspects of life itself."[4]

Supreme Court opinions are as authoritative as the words of the Constitution itself, and they bind litigants as well as judges. The most powerful constitutional claims, then, are those that throw the Supreme Court's words into the face of any lower court that must heed them. It is simple, for example, after the Supreme Court has already struck down a Virginia law prohibiting interracial marriage,[5] to make the case that an identical law in Kentucky must also be invalid. A claimant would only need to file a lawsuit against Kentucky citing the Virginia case, and telling the judge, "the Supreme Court said here that the Constitution means people are free to marry outside their own race." And, on the Supreme Court's authority, the lower court would be obliged to void the Kentucky law. The Supreme Court is bound as well as the lower courts by its past decisions. The principle of *stare decisis* (a Latin phrase meaning "a matter decided") requires that the Supreme Court respect and abide by its own precedent except in very rare circumstances. It is a principle the Supreme Court takes very seriously; of the tens of thousands of decisions the Court has made over the past two centuries, it has overturned fewer than 200.

Although it is simple to make the case for an established right like the right to marry, it is much harder, in contrast, to make a "case of first impression," that is, to ask a court to protect a right that has never yet been recognized. The Texas abortion law challenged in *Roe v. Wade* had been on the books for 115 years, but no one had ever before suggested that statutes outlawing abortion violate the Constitution. Sarah Weddington and Linda Coffee had to draw upon the Court's pronouncements on other topics to make their case, and try to show that what the Court had said in these opinions led inevitably to a favorable decision in their case.

They set to work in the law library, drafting arguments for the legal brief they would file in federal court. Judges read briefs from both sides of a case to familiarize themselves beforehand with the points the attorneys will make and the authorities they will cite when they argue the case in court. Sarah and Linda began by combing the Constitution for words or phrases that could be interpreted as protecting the right to abortion. The First Amendment, they noted, guarantees freedom of association. This, they claimed, had to include the freedom of a doctor to advise a pregnant patient to seek medical treatment that she wanted and was in her best interest. The Texas abortion law, they asserted, interfered with this right by preventing doctors from recommending abortion in cases where pregnancy jeopardized their patients' health.

The Fourth and Fifth Amendments, protecting citizens from unlawful searches and forced confessions, they argued, showed the Constitution's more general concern with dignity, privacy, and security. Texas's interference with such a personal matter as abortion, they urged, contradicted these constitutional values.

The Fourteenth Amendment's promise of "liberty," they claimed, included a woman's liberty to decide for herself whether to terminate her pregnancy. Finally, they pointed to the Ninth Amendment, which says "the enumeration in the Constitution of certain rights shall not be construed to deny or disparage others retained by the people." This statement, they argued, plainly means that the Constitution's short list of rights is not exhaustive; there are other, important rights not mentioned in the document that cannot be abridged by any state. A woman's right to choose abortion, they argued, is one such right.

✳   Sarah found a line of cases going back to the World War I era, in which the Supreme Court vigorously defended the right to a kind of family privacy that is not explicitly mentioned in the Constitution. These cases, she argued, supported their claim that the state could not interfere with a woman's abortion decision.

The first two of these decisions had invalidated laws that interfered with✳parents' right to educate their children as they saw fit. *Meyer v. Nebraska*[6] addressed a challenge by a German teacher, Meyer, to a Nebraska law that made it illegal to teach foreign languages to children before the eighth grade. The prohibition had been passed in the wake of the nation's struggle with Germany in the Great War, and it was aimed at suppressing the culture of Nebraska's German minority.[7]

The Court struck down the Nebraska law, saying it violated the Fourteenth Amendment's promise of liberty. "Without doubt," the Court held, liberty means "not merely freedom from bodily restraint but also the right of the individual . . . to engage in any of the common occupations of life, to acquire useful knowledge, to marry, establish a home and bring up children, . . . and generally to enjoy those privileges long recognized . . . as essential to the orderly pursuit of happiness by free men."[8]

Two years later, in *Pierce v. Society of Sisters*,[9] the Court struck down an Oregon law, rooted in hostility toward the state's Catholic population, that would have compelled all students to attend public schools and shut down both parochial and secular private schools. Again, the Court cited the Fourteenth Amendment right to liberty, which included the right "of parents and guardians to direct the upbringing and education of children under their control."[10] "Government has no power, the Court said in these cases, 'to standardize its children' or to 'foster a homogeneous people.'"[11] *Meyer* and *Pierce* are the "immediate ancestors" of the liberty interest that, the Supreme Court would declare in *Roe*, encompasses a woman's decision whether to terminate her pregnancy.[12]

The Supreme Court issued other privacy decisions, touching more closely on the question of abortion, in later years. In 1942, a new "science" called eugenics (from Greek words meaning "good genes") had come into vogue. The theory behind eugenics was that criminal tendencies are inherited, as are eye color or hair color. From this theory, it followed that criminal adults would naturally spawn criminal offspring.

The theory is now discredited, and the "science" it supported has fallen out of favor. But the Supreme Court's encounter with eugenics-based policy gave Sarah and Linda some powerful language for their brief. In 1942, the state of Oklahoma had passed a law mandating the sterilization of anyone convicted two or more times of "felonies involving moral turpitude."[13] Skinner, a convicted robber and chicken thief, sued the state in order to avoid being castrated. The Supreme Court struck down the Oklahoma law in ✳*Skinner v. Oklahoma*. Justice Douglas wrote for the majority, "We are dealing here with legislation which involves one of the basic civil rights of man. Marriage and procreation are fundamental to the very existence and survival of the race. [There] is no redemption for the individual whom the law touches. . . . He is forever deprived of a basic liberty."[14]

Skinner was a very significant precedent for the argument Sarah and Linda would make in *Roe* because the Constitution is generally understood to secure so-called negative rights. That is, it does not help or encourage so much as it prevents the government from hindering or discouraging our exercise of certain freedoms. The First Amendment, for instance, promises freedom of religious belief. This means not only that we are free to worship the god we choose; it means that we need not worship *any* god. Government simply has no say in the matter. In the same way, the Court's recognition in *Skinner* of a constitutional right to procreate implied the existence of a right *not* to procreate—the right ultimately recognized in *Roe*. *Skinner* opened the door for a claimant to argue that the State could not constitutionally force childbearing any more than it could force sterilization.

✳ Finally, Weddington stumbled onto a 1965 case that contained the Court's plainest acknowledgment yet of a constitutional right to privacy in matters related to marriage, family, and sex. *Griswold v. Connecticut* struck down a Connecticut law that made illegal the use of birth control by married couples. Estelle Griswold, the executive director of Planned

*Estelle Griswold (left), executive director of a
Planned Parenthood clinic in New Haven,
Connecticut, celebrates the Supreme Court's 1965
decision that struck down a Connecticut statute
that outlawed the use of contraceptives by married
couples.* Griswold v. Connecticut *was a key
legal precedent for* Roe v. Wade.

Parenthood of Connecticut, had been arrested after
she gave contraceptives to a married couple, and was
convicted as an accessory to the crime of using birth
control. The Supreme Court declared the law unconstitutional even though the Constitution makes no
mention of marriage or birth control.

Griswold said, in essence, that the Constitution
presupposes a class of rights that are so fundamental
as to constitute the bedrock of a free society. The right
to marital privacy, the Court held, fell into that class.

Justice William O. Douglas wrote for the majority, "We deal with a right of privacy older than the Bill of Rights—older than our political parties, older than our school system. Marriage is a coming together for better or for worse, hopefully enduring, and intimate to the degree of being sacred."

The Fourteenth Amendment's promise of liberty, the Court explained, would be meaningless if it did not protect the citizen from intrusions by the State into matters as personal as sexual intimacy in marriage. Justice Arthur J. Goldberg wrote in a concurring opinion:

The makers of our Constitution undertook to secure conditions favorable to the pursuit of happiness. They recognized the significance of man's spiritual nature, of his feelings and of his intellect. They knew that only a part of the pain, pleasure and satisfactions of life are to be found in material things. They sought to protect Americans in their beliefs, their thoughts, their emotions and their sensations. They conferred, as against the Government, the right to be let alone—the most comprehensive of rights and the right most valued by civilized men.

If *Skinner* opened the door to *Roe* by announcing a right to procreate, *Griswold* crossed the threshold by announcing a right to have sex without procreating. Beyond the threshold, Weddington and Coffee would argue, the Constitution held open a room of privacy where a pregnant woman could decide for herself whether to abort or carrry her pregnancy to term. The two lawyers waited breathlessly for their court date.

Chapter 5

CHANGING TIMES

It does not take the Supreme Court to get rid of a bad law. A law, at least in theory, expresses the will of a majority that can change its mind in changing times. The people can lobby their elected representatives to repeal or rewrite a disfavored or outdated law, arguing that the law no longer reflects their will. The idea is that the same majoritarian force that enshrines a popular opinion in law can jettison or modify the opinion and, therefore, the law at a later date.

Advocates of freer access to abortion fought for their vision at the polls as well as in the courts. A court victory, they knew, would mean instantaneous vindication of their point of view. Legislatures would simply no longer be free to pass laws prohibiting abortion once such laws were declared unconstitutional. But reform advocates also recognized the power of a persuaded majority and the controversy that could ignite if the courts imposed a rule of law on a community that was unprepared to accept it.

In 1960, abortion was a criminal offense in every state in the nation, prohibited by laws like the one Texas passed in the 1800s. By 1965, however, moved by tragedy and progress, the country was rethinking this position. Thalidomide and rubella first brought abortion into the national media in the early sixties.

Thalidomide, a tranquilizer banned in the United

States but sold in Europe, had been used by thousands of women before it was discovered that the drug caused dramatic birth defects when taken by pregnant women. European women who ingested the drug during pregnancy in the late 1950s and early 1960s had borne infants "with seallike flippers instead of arms or with shortened thighs and twisted legs. Others were missing ears or had paralyzed faces."[1]

In 1962, Sherri Finkbine, a 29-year-old mother of four and a popular television hostess on the children's show "Romper Room," read about Thalidomide in her local newspaper, the *Arizona Republic*. She was three months pregnant and had, over the past few months, used a number of headache pills that her husband had brought back from a trip to England. The newspaper story made her wonder about the medication she had taken, and she called her doctor and asked him to check on the pills. The next day, he called her back with terrible news: not only had she taken Thalidomide, but it was the strongest possible dosage. He told her there was a serious chance that her pregnancy would result in a badly deformed child.

Arizona prohibited abortion except in cases where a medical committee certified that pregnancy threatened the life of the mother. Finkbine's doctor assured her that, if she sought an abortion under the circumstances, the hospital's committee would grant her request. As promised, the board approved Finkbine's not-technically-legal abortion, and she was booked into the operating room for eight o'clock the following Monday morning.

Over the weekend, however, Finkbine became concerned about how easy it had been for her to get hold of a drug that had destroyed her pregnancy. Worried that other women would unknowingly do the same thing, she telephoned a friend who worked for the *Republic*, and by Monday morning, under the head-

*Fearing that their unborn child would be badly
deformed, Bob and Sherri Finkbine prepare to jet to
Sweden for an abortion in August 1962. When
publicity about Finkbine's situation caused
a U.S. hospital to cancel her scheduled abortion,
she went abroad to terminate her pregnancy.*

line "Baby-Deforming Drug May Cost Woman Her
Child Here," she was front-page news. Fearing that
the publicity would provoke a criminal investigation,
the hospital canceled Finkbine's scheduled abortion.[2]

Wire services picked up the story immediately,
and Finkbine and her husband, Bob, were hounded by

reporters. Thousands of cards and letters, some containing death threats against her and her children, poured in, and the FBI was called in to protect her.[3] Finally, the Finkbines released a statement saying, "We have concluded to seek help in a more favorable legal climate."[4] They flew to Sweden where, early in the fourth month of her pregnancy, Sherri had an abortion. "As she came out of the anaesthetic, the obstetrician told her that the embryo was so seriously deformed it would never have survived."[5]

Bob later estimated that the protracted and difficult ordeal had cost them $4,000. As the Finkbines packed to return home, Vatican Radio denounced them and called Sherri's decision "a crime." "Crime is the only possible definition," the Vatican declared, because "the victim was a human being."[6]

The following month, a Gallup poll posed the question: "As you may have heard or read, an American woman recently had a legal abortion in Sweden after having taken the drug Thalidomide, which has been linked to birth defects. Do you think this woman did the right thing or the wrong thing in having this abortion operation?" Fifty-two percent of all the people who responded answered that Finkbine had done the right thing. Only thirty-two percent said she had done the wrong thing.[7]

An outbreak of rubella, or German measles, between 1962 and 1965 focused national attention on abortion once again. When contracted by a woman during early pregnancy, rubella can cause blindness, deafness, and severe mental retardation in the fetus. California suffered a particularly severe epidemic in 1964, and many doctors at prominent hospitals routinely performed abortions on women who had been exposed in spite of California's law that, like Arizona's, permitted abortion only in cases where pregnancy threatened the mother's life.

In 1966, the head of the California State Board of

Medical Examiners, a devout Catholic, publicly threatened to "get" any physician who performed an abortion merely because of maternal exposure to rubella. Soon afterward, the board fulfilled this threat, charging nine physicians, who became known as the San Francisco Nine, with performing illegal abortions on women exposed to rubella. The reaction of the medical community was swift and sharp. "Physicians . . . across the country rallied to send money and support to their threatened colleagues. Some 2,000 physicians formed a nationwide support group, which included the deans of most of the major medical schools in the country."[8]

The combined forces of the medical and feminist communities succeeded in reforming California's law in 1967. The new statute enlarged the exceptions to the criminal prohibition in California, allowing doctors to perform abortions where pregnancy would gravely impair the physical or mental health of the woman. It also permitted the abortion of pregnancies resulting from rape or incest.[9]

Three years later, in Minnesota, when the legislature stopped short of passing a repeal bill, Dr. Jane Hodgson resolved to test the state's traditional criminal abortion law. At fifty-five, Hodgson had practiced for twenty-two years as St. Paul's only female gynecologist, and had served for three years, with a growing sense of frustration, on the State Medical Association's Ad Hoc Abortion Committee. When she met Nancy Widmyer, a young housewife with three children, and confirmed that Widmyer had contracted rubella during her first month of pregnancy, she knew her hour had arrived. Hodgson sought formal confirmation from three other doctors that a therapeutic abortion was appropriate in Widmyer's case. Then she filed a suit in federal court challenging the Minnesota criminal abortion law. When the court delayed, Hodgson acted. The fetus she aborted in a hospital

In 1970, Minnesota gynecologist Jane Hodgson became the first U.S. physician to be arrested for performing a medically approved abortion in a hospital.

was severely deformed.[10] Dr. Hodgson announced to the press on April 29 that she had terminated Widmyer's pregnancy and, on May 19, 1970, she made headlines by becoming the first licensed physician in American history to be criminally charged for performing a medically approved hospital abortion.[11] After a lengthy trial, she was convicted and sentenced to a suspended sentence of thirty days in prison. The Minnesota legislature later changed the penalty for performing illegal abortions to life imprisonment.[12]

The truth is that there had been an unspoken agreement between law enforcement and medical professionals that, as long as no one got hurt, prosecutors would not second-guess a doctor's opinion that an abortion was "necessary" in a given case. Zad Leavy, a young district attorney in Los Angeles County, had published an article in 1959 in the *Los Angeles Bar Journal* in which he had exposed this charade and called for liberalization of California's abortion law. Leavy's first assignment with the DA's office had been to prosecute abortion cases, and he had quickly learned "how much suffering was going on" in the underground world of illegal abortion. He also soon discovered, through meeting so many uncooperative witnesses, that "women were very grateful to good abortionists." Leavy's article said "It is common knowledge among medical men as well as legal authorities that only a small percentage of therapeutic abortions performed today are legal."[13]

The year after Jane Hodgson's arrest, with *Roe* pending in the federal courts, the Texas legislature held hearings on a bill to reform the state's criminal abortion law. No one had high hopes the bill would pass, but the hearings drew out in force advocates on both sides of the debate. Sarah Weddington tells the following story:

The most moving testimony was given by . . . an unforgettable, gutsy woman, the sole provider for her two children, who knew that another child would have made it impossible for her family to survive. She would have lost her job and would not have been able to sup-

port the three children financially. "I could not have that baby," the woman said in a steely voice, tears streaming down her face.

The hearing room was completely silent as she told how night after night, when her children were asleep, she would take the heaviest book in the house and whack her stomach repeatedly. For hours she would sit and pummel her belly. And now she relived those nights in her testimony, her face cringing in pain. . . . She described the welts that resulted on her stomach and the bruises on her skin. She continued the beating until one night she felt cramps: she had succeeded—at the cost of great pain and suffering, she had succeeded.[14]

Pat Maginnis, founder of the Citizens' Committee for Humane Abortion Laws, described an experience that forged her convictions in a 1973 book, *Abortion II*, by Lawrence Lader. As a medical technician stationed in the Panama Canal Zone for the Women's Army Corps, Maginnis reported, "I saw the brutality of the system—a soldier's wife who had attempted suicide after being refused an abortion, held captive like an animal in the hospital ward, literally forced by the staff to continue a pregnancy she hated."[15]

During the years that dramas like these were being played out in the national press, women were entering the American workforce in unprecedented numbers. They found themselves competing with men for jobs in which their chances for promotion or advancement depended on service uninterrupted by the demands of maternity or child care. Women's experience at work, where men consistently received better pay and treatment, convinced many that control of fertility and reproduction were critical to the achievement of equality in the labor market.[16]

At the same time, population control had become a prominent social issue. In 1954, a biologist named Paul Ehrlich published a famous pamphlet, *The Population Bomb*, in which he wrote that population "threatens to create an explosion as disruptive and dangerous as the explosion of the atom." Poverty and mortality rates in the developing nations, with which the United States had increasing contact after 1950, seemed to prove what theorists like Ehrlich suggested: that a low birthrate was essential to a nation's economic prosperity and well-being. It is a measure of the country's interest and concern with the issue that former Presidents Harry Truman and Dwight Eisenhower became cochairmen of Planned Parenthood/World Population in 1965.[17]

Starting in 1967, several states broadened the "therapeutic" exception to their criminal abortion prohibitions to allow abortions to preserve the life or health of the woman. Some, like California, also made exceptions in cases of rape or incest. In 1970, Hawaii and New York became the first states to repeal their criminal abortion laws outright.

But the same year also showed the first signs of an ascending counterforce. President Nixon publicly declared that abortion was "an unacceptable form of population control" and announced his "personal belief in the sanctity of human life—including the life of the yet unborn."[18] In 1971, John C. Willke, a Cincinnati physician and the father of the National Right to Life Committee, published a *Handbook on Abortion* listing compelling reasons to oppose abortion and featuring grisly pictures of fetuses aborted in advanced stages of pregnancy.[19] As Willke presents them, the arguments against abortion are wonderfully simple. The life of a human being begins at the moment of conception, he maintains, and there is no scientific, rational, or moral justification for believing otherwise. Abortion, in his view, is just a euphemism for murder. And although murder in some circumstances may be justified, it is utterly indefensible to take the life of the weakest and most innocent human being for the mere convenience of another.

By 1972, antiabortion forces, following the energetic leadership of the Roman Catholic church, "had repeal advocates badly outgunned despite" public opinion polls showing that a solid majority favored relaxing the traditional prohibitions on abortion.[20] That year, Willke helped defeat a Michigan referendum that would have legalized abortion in the first twenty weeks of pregnancy. On October 5, 1972, a *Detroit News* poll showed that 59 percent supported the measure,[21] but one month later, on November 7, the referendum lost by a vote of 61 percent to 39 percent.[22] Catholic parishes throughout the state had passed the basket to help fund pro-life activists in Michigan,[23] and in the final weeks before the vote, they carpeted the state with Willke's glossy new brochure, *Life and Death*. The brochure, whose cover contrasted a color photograph of a premature infant born at twenty-one weeks of pregnancy with a grisly one of a fetus aborted by saline injection, was distributed to most of the two million households in the state. On the same day that the Michigan referendum went down in defeat, Willke's brochure helped achieve a similar outcome in North Dakota, where it was even more widely distributed and where a referendum on abortion lost by an even wider margin.[24] Soon after, Pennsylvania *toughened* its criminal abortion law, passing a measure that would have barred any abortion except where three doctors declared it necessary to save a woman's life; this law was stopped only by the governor's veto.[25]

In short, the Right to Life movement effectively arrested what had seemed to be a tidal shift in public opinion. In 1973 only four states, Hawaii, New York, Washington, and Alaska, guaranteed a woman the right to decide for herself whether to terminate her pregnancy. Attempts to repeal criminal abortion laws had been defeated in Montana, New Mexico, Iowa, Minnesota, Maryland, Colorado, and Massachusetts.[26] Between 1971 and 1973 not a single additional state moved to repeal its criminal prohibition on abortion early in pregnancy.[27]

The legislative solution was fizzling, not only because of the discouraging blows meted out in the states where the fervent Right to Life movement had organized, but precisely *because* it was now possible for women who had the money to obtain safe abortions by traveling to one of a handful of other states. The availability of abortion to upper- and middle-class women diminished their incentive to take part in an increasingly ugly political fracas to win the right to do locally something they considered profoundly private. The women for whom the incentive remained were those too poor to travel and, therefore, least able to take advantage of the new laws in foreign states. But poor women wielded the least political power to change the laws in their home states. The legal status of abortion before *Roe* had become like the legal status of slavery before the Thirteenth Amendment: some states allowed it and some forbade it. A woman's right to choose stood or fell depending on where she was and where she could get to.

It may seem strange that it took the Supreme Court, the *antimajoritarian* branch of our government, finally to enshrine in law what every public opinion poll showed was the majority's preference for freer access to abortion. But the struggle for abortion reform shows how the reality of politics can diverge from the theory, which presumes that law will express the majority's values. "A small but intense minority can exercise political influence disproportionate to its numbers when a diffuse and silent majority does not organize to fight back. . . . [T]he legislative success of the Catholic Church leadership and its disciplined parishioners [w]as a textbook case of this phenomenon."[28]

In 1970, in addition to *Roe v. Wade* in Texas, abortion cases were wending their way through the federal courts in Georgia, Colorado, Illinois, Indiana, Kentucky, Michigan, Minnesota, New Jersey, North Carolina, Oregon, and Vermont. The Supreme Court seemed bound to hear one of them.

But by that time, at least one advocate of legal reform suspected that not even the Supreme Court would be able to put such a mighty controversy to rest. A spokesman for the Association for the Study of Abortion, a citizens group founded in the sixties to lobby for the repeal of criminal abortion laws, confessed to a reporter for the Associated Press, "Now that I have seen the fierceness of the opposition, I no longer feel [that a] favorable ruling" from the Supreme Court would mean the struggle "would be over. Instead of it being the end," it would represent only "the beginning of a tough new era."[29]

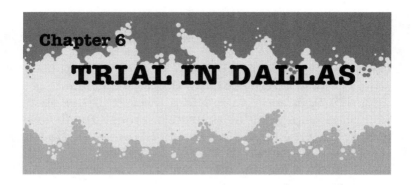

Chapter 6

TRIAL IN DALLAS

The afternoon of May 22, 1970, found Sarah Weddington and Linda Coffee seated at a long table on the fourth floor of the Dallas federal courthouse waiting for the three judges who would hear their case to assemble. Luck had smiled on them. Their panel included Coffee's former boss, Judge Sarah T. Hughes, as well as Judges William Taylor and Irving Goldberg. Taylor was known for his fairness, and Goldberg, for his brilliance. Judge Hughes was a woman light-years ahead of her time. She had been a state court judge in Dallas for twenty-six years before she was picked for the federal bench in 1961. She had won the appointment over the other local contender, Dallas County DA Henry Wade.

At all of five feet tall, Judge Hughes had been elected three times to the Texas state legislature before she became a judge in 1935. She had earned her law degree from George Washington University in the 1920s by taking classes at night while working during the day as a policewoman. With her husband, George, she had moved to Dallas in 1924, and she immediately launched a long and illustrious career in law and politics. Judge Hughes won minor national fame when her name came up in nomination for the vice presidency at the 1952 Democratic National Convention. Throughout her career, she had been an outspoken champion of women's rights, but most of the country knew Judge Hughes as the woman who had administered the presidential oath of office to Lyndon B. Johnson on Air Force One as the plane carried John F. Kennedy's body back to Washington, D.C., on the afternoon of November 22, 1963.[1]

A new plaintiff, Dr. James Hubert Hallford, had joined the lawsuit. Dr. Hallford had been indicted on two felony counts of having performed abortions in his small-town office in Carrollton, Texas. The two local policemen who handled criminal investigations for Carrollton's sixteen-member force had noticed an "odd traffic" of college-aged women arriving each day at Hallford's office just off the town square, and in due time, Hallford had been arrested. His attorney, Fred Bruner, planned to challenge the constitutionality of the Texas abortion law as part of Hallford's criminal defense, and when he heard about Coffee's lawsuit, he contacted her at once. Linda and Sarah, for their part, were delighted to have a medical plaintiff, as well as some additional legal help.[2]

Hallford's complaint stated that his abortion patients included rape and incest victims, as well as women who had cancer or who had been exposed to rubella. He asserted that Texas's abortion law was unconstitutionally vague; it's sole exception allowed abortions necessary to "save the life of the mother," but it gave doctors no guidance about when they could safely assert that pregnancy threatened a woman's life. Was it enough, for example, if the woman was determined to commit suicide if she could not have an abortion? If her life would be shortened by continuing the pregnancy, or only if she was sure to die imminently?

Bruner's junior partner, Roy Merrill, wondering whether Hallford had operated this underground sideline to his medical practice just for the money, once asked his client what he thought of abortion. "It's not an issue for me," Hallford had answered. During his medical training, Hallford explained, he had seen scores of women admitted to Dallas' Parkland Memorial Hospital who had been injured by amateur abortionists. So, "it's real, real easy for me," Hallford said, "because when a woman comes to me, by the time I ever see her, she's already made up her mind: she's going to have an abortion. . . . It's just a question of who's going to do it."[3]

Beside adding Hallford, Weddington and Coffee had finally resolved their fears of mootness by amending the lawsuit to be a class action. Jane Roe was due to give birth within a few months of the trial date. By converting her case to an action on behalf of all women "similarly situated," they hoped to short-circuit Wade's argument that Roe's giving birth would extinguish the "case or controversy" at the heart of the lawsuit. The idea behind the class action was that there would always be one "Jane Roe" or another who was pregnant in the state of Texas, and thwarted in her pursuit of an abortion by the Texas penal code.

The panel filed in, and the attorneys rose and stood in deference until the judges were seated. At Goldberg's nod, Coffee began. She said that she would address the procedural issues and Weddington would address the constitutional issues in the case. In order to show their standing to sue the state, she began by describing the circumstances of the various plaintiffs and how the criminal abortion law affected them. Next, she canvassed the constitutional limitations— established by the First, Fourth, Fifth, Ninth, and Fourteenth Amendments—that she believed the Texas law exceeded. The judges were not interested in hearing about the First Amendment; they asked Coffee to tell them about the Ninth, which says: "The enumeration in the Constitution of certain rights shall not be construed to deny or disparage others retained by the people." Coffee responded by pointing to the line of cases that recognized certain "fundamental" rights—the right to marry, to procreate, and to raise children—that the Constitution did not mention. The right to abortion, she asserted, was on par with those rights.

When it was Weddington's turn to speak, her voice shook. She was twenty-five years old. A few uncontested divorces for friends, a dozen simple wills, and an adoption for a family member represented the sum of her legal experience. Judge Hughes looked at her reassuringly from the bench and made a slight wink. Weddington calmed down. The crux of her argument was that the law had never treated the fetus as a person. She began listing cases to prove the point, but Goldberg interrupted. He asked Weddington to suppose the court recognized a Ninth Amendment right to abortion. Then, "could you think of any compelling state interest that would justify interfering with that right?" Weddington recognized this recitation of the test courts use to decide when a legislature may trespass on a constitutional right. Goldberg's point was that constitutional rights are not absolute. They can be abridged by regulations in situations where the State shows a compelling interest in regulating. Prohibitions on yelling "fire!" in a crowded theater, for example, infringe the right to free speech, but they are not unconstitutional in light of the government's compelling interest in order and public safety. Goldberg wondered whether women's privacy was all that was at stake in the abortion context or if a state could assert a compelling counter interest that justified some regulation.

Weddington responded that she believed the state's only valid interest in abortion was in protecting women's health. On that ground, she asserted, a state could require that only licensed physicians perform

Federal District Judge Sarah T. Hughes,
pictured here in 1972, sat on the three-judge
panel that made the original ruling for the
plaintiffs in Roe. v. Wade.

abortions. Still, Goldberg pressed. Did it make any difference how far along a woman was in her pregnancy?
Finally, Weddington conceded, "The state of pregnancy
gives me some pause," and she followed by saying, "You
could recognize life when the fetus is able to live out-

side the body of the mother," somewhere between five-and-a-half and seven months of pregnancy.[4]

Fred Bruner devoted his share of the allotted time to arguing that the law was too vague to be constitutional.

Jay Floyd, the assistant chief of the state attorney general's office, stood to argue Texas's side of the case. He began by saying that none of the plaintiffs had standing. Jane Roe, if she was still pregnant, was too far along to get an abortion now, and the Doe couple's fear of conceiving was too remote an injury to give them a stake in the controversy. The panel did not seem persuaded by Floyd's standing arguments. Goldberg reminded him that some of the children involved in the school desegregation cases had graduated from college by the time the courts heard their claims. Did that mean they didn't have a right to attend desegregated schools? And Judge Hughes pointed out that, if the panel adopted Floyd's position, no one would ever have standing to litigate an abortion case that went on longer than the nine months it takes for a human fetus to gestate.

Floyd, sensing that he would not win on this point, moved on to rebut Sarah's constitutional arguments. He said that he didn't see how the right to free speech or equal protection had anything to do with abortion, and the panel seemed to agree. But Goldberg pressed him, as he had pressed the others, on the Ninth Amendment and vagueness claims.

John Tolle, from Henry Wade's office, presented the second part of Texas's defense. His argument was straightforward. "The state has got a right to protect life that is in being at whatever stage it may be in being," he asserted, and the state's approach to protecting fetal life "is a matter for legislative determination." Once a pregnancy begins, he claimed, "the right of that child to life is superior to that woman's right to privacy."[5]

Before the hearing adjourned, Goldberg had one more question for Weddington. "Henry Wade is only the district attorney for Dallas County," he pointed out. "If the panel does decide to enjoin Wade from enforcing the abortion statute," Goldberg asked, "what would stop all the other district attorneys in all the other counties in the state from continuing to prosecute offenders?" At this Sarah hesitated, flushed. "We goofed," she answered, and laughter filled the courtroom as the hearing ended.[6]

In less than four weeks, the panel announced its decision. Coffee's voice was so calm when she telephoned on June 17 that it took a moment for Weddington to take in that they had won. The opinion was straightforward, not ten pages long, but it gave the plaintiffs almost everything they had asked for. The panel ruled that the Does lacked standing, but that Jane Roe and Dr. Hallford, as well as the classes each represented, were both sufficiently invested in the controversy to assert a legal challenge to the Texas law. The opinion went on:

> *[The plaintiffs assert that the Texas law] deprive[s] single women and married couples of their right, secured by the Ninth Amendment, to choose whether to have children. We agree. The essence of the interest sought to be protected here is the right of choice over events which, by their character and consequences, bear in a fundamental manner on the privacy of individuals. . . . [The] freedom to choose in the matter of abortions has been accorded the status of a 'fundamental' right in every case coming to the attention of this Court where the question has been raised.*

The panel went on to acknowledge that there were compelling reasons for a state to regulate abortion, including the state's interests in ensuring that abortions were performed by qualified practitioners in appropriate surroundings. The trouble with the Texas law, the panel declared, was that it went well beyond promoting these interests by outlawing almost all abortions. For these reasons, the panel concluded, the law was unconstitutional. Weddington and Coffee's only disappointment was that the panel stopped short of enjoining Henry Wade from enforcing the law, and they resolved to appeal this part of the decision.[7]

The *Roe* ruling made news all over the country. Weddington and Coffee shook their heads and laughed over the final line in a story that appeared in the *Houston Post*: "If their day in court proves anything, it certainly proves that genteel Southern ladies can indeed be very good lawyers." Most surprising was the statement of Mrs. Peter J. Collora, the president of Catholic Women of the Dallas Diocese, quoted in the *Dallas Times-Herald*. Collora said, "I have great faith and trust in our courts. . . . [T]his decision is the only one the court could have made. You couldn't prosecute under those terms. They really were too vague and too broad. Why have a law you can't enforce?"[10] Less surprising, Henry Wade announced to the Dallas press that he would appeal the ruling and that, because the court had not ordered otherwise, his office would continue to prosecute those who broke the law. Of course, his announcement left in limbo all the women in Dallas county who wanted abortions and all the doctors who wanted to provide them; the court had said the law was void, but the DA had promised to arrest anyone who acted on the court's word. The good news was that Wade's public statement that he would carry on in the face of the panel's declaration that the law was unconstitutional sped *Roe* to the Supreme Court.

Ordinarily, an appeal of a federal trial court's decision is made to an intermediate federal court of appeal, commonly known as a circuit court, which must render a decision before a dissatisfied party can seek relief from the Supreme Court. But in the special case where a lower federal court has held a state law unconstitutional and local authorities have vowed to enforce it anyway, it is possible to appeal directly to the Supreme Court. Henry Wade's announcement made *Roe* just such a case.

A party who has lost or partially lost a case in a state supreme court or a federal circuit court has the right to file a petition for a hearing before the justices of the U.S. Supreme Court. The justices have no obligation to hear these appeals; they pick only those that raise important, disputed issues involving federal law or the U.S. Constitution. Of the thousands of appeals the Court is asked to hear every year, fewer than 100 win a review, which means that the cases will be argued before the justices and decided with a written opinion.[11] Henry Wade appealed the trial court's ruling that the Texas law was unconstitutional, and Sarah and Linda appealed the court's failure to enjoin (prevent enforcement of) the law. With other abortion cases pending in the federal courts of Georgia, Colorado, Illinois, Indiana, Kentucky, Michigan, Minnesota, New Jersey, North Carolina, Oregon, and Vermont, it was impossible to guess which the Supreme Court would agree to consider. The early months of 1971 found Sarah and Linda again waiting for news.

Norma McCorvey, meanwhile, had slipped into a blacker depression than she had ever known. After signing the papers Weddington and Coffee had prepared to make her a plaintiff in *Roe v. Wade*, she had gone home and waited. She didn't hear much from her lawyers, though.

Henry McCluskey called her at her father's apartment faithfully every week or two to tell her the case was moving along. He reminded her every time he called that he would be glad to arrange an adoption if the lawsuit didn't work. And every time, McCorvey would rail at him. She knew as surely as she knew her own name that she couldn't survive having another child—she couldn't take care of it, and she couldn't give it up either.[12]

She fled the long, empty days in her father's apartment for friends she had known as a drifter in Oaklawn, the part of Dallas where the hippies congregated. Her friends had disappeared, but others—laidback, passive, and zoned out—welcomed her. She "discovered that if [she] smoked enough dope and drank enough wine, it was possible not to think about being pregnant."[13] Once she checked in with Henry and found him frantic. He told her that her case was about to go to trial, and Sarah and Linda needed her to sign an affidavit. She hitched a ride to Linda's office, signed the papers, and returned to Oaklawn. McCorvey would later write that she "was invisible again. And stayed invisible, burying myself in drugs and alcohol, as Linda and Sarah made history in my name."[14]

By the time the trial ended, Norma was six months pregnant. When she called in a month later, Coffee told her to come right over. When Norma arrived, she told her the good news: they had won. And then she told her the bad news: it was still impossible to get a legal abortion in Texas. Norma felt her world crumbling. She was beside herself. "But Norma," Linda said, "what does it matter? It's too late for you anyway. You can't get an abortion after the first six months."[15] By the time she left, McCorvey was furious. She felt she had been led on. She called Henry McCluskey and told him to arrange an adoption. Then she moved back into her father's apartment to await the birth of her third child.

The pains came in the middle of the night. She

woke up her father, and he drove her to the hospital. The baby was born almost immediately, and just like the last time, the nurses whisked it away before she could see it. When McCorvey woke up, it was daylight. A nurse bustled in with a needle. "Time for your shot!" she announced, explaining that it was to dry up her breast milk since Norma wasn't keeping her baby. Later in the afternoon, another nurse walked in, carrying a blanketed bundle. "Feeding time!" she said. Then she handed Norma her baby. Norma panicked. She recalled

It was like getting a glimpse of hell, all my shame and fear and guilt and love and sadness all rolled up into a ball and placed in front of me.

Was this my baby? Why were they giving it to me? Should I look at it? Or not look at it?

I was too full of pain to say anything. Through the blanket, I could feel the baby moving. Breathing.

There was a flap of cloth over its face. My entire body, my entire soul cried out to me to turn the flap down, to look at my baby's face. But my mind told me that it would be the worst thing I could ever do.

My mind won. My heart lost. I never touched the flap. I felt sick to my stomach. I started crying, loudly, in pure despair.

The nurse must have seen the expression on my face, because she quickly realized she'd done something awful and ran out of the room. I was left alone with the baby, paralyzed, for another minute or two.

The nurse rushed back in, this time with two orderlies. She pulled the baby out of my arms and handed it to an orderly, who left.

Then the baby was gone forever. The nurse didn't say anything to me. She looked scared. She turned to the orderly, who was still standing next to her, and pointed at me.

"You can watch her for me, can't you?" she said to him. He nodded.

"Get out!" I cried, with all the strength I could manage. They both turned and walked out and left me alone. Then I turned my face to the wall and wept.[16]

McCorvey got drunk her first night out of the hospital. And, as soon as she was thin enough to get back into her old clothes, she went out to bars and got drunk every night. She spent her days alone in her father's apartment. She slept, she cried, she walked the streets, she drank. And finally, she knew what she had to do.

Taking every loose dollar and stray nickel she could find in the house, she walked outside to find the neighborhood drug dealers. She bought every kind of pill they had. When her father got home, she cooked him supper, cleaned the dishes, and fell into bed to wait for morning. After her father left for work, Norma took her last five dollars and bought a bottle of Wild Turkey. It was the first time she felt strong in months. Finally, she would be free. She drank down the dozens of pills she had bought until she began to hallucinate. Then she lost consciousness.

She woke up the following afternoon in her father's room, and she knew she had failed. But there sat her father beside the bed, looking more worried than he had ever looked. He had stayed home from work to watch over her.

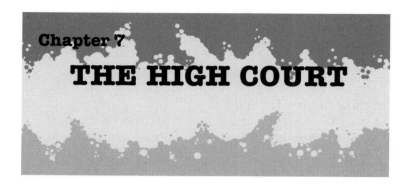

Chapter 7

THE HIGH COURT

On May 21, 1971, the Orders of the Supreme Court included the following inscrutable notice:

> *No. 808. ROE ET AL. V. WADE. Appeal from D.C.N.D.Tex. Probable jurisdiction postponed to hearing of case on the merits. Reported below: 314 F.Supp. 1217.*
> *No. 971. DOE ET AL. V. BOLTON, ATTORNEY GENERAL OF GEORGIA, ET AL. Appeal from D.C.N.D. Ga. Probable jurisdiction postponed to hearing of case on the merits. Reported below: 319 F.Supp. 10481*[1]

Weddington and Coffee exulted. The Supreme Court had granted their petition to hear argument in *Roe v. Wade!*

Doe v. Bolton, the other argument that would be scheduled for the same day, was an abortion case out of Georgia whose progress the two lawyers had been following over the months. The Georgia law challenged in *Doe* represented the less extreme variation on the criminal prohibitions that regulated abortion in most states. Whereas the harsh Texas law allowed abortion only to "save the life" of the woman, the Georgia law permitted abortion when continuing a pregnancy jeopardized a woman's life or threatened serious and permanent injury to her health; when the fetus was likely

78

to be born with a grave, permanent, and incurable defect; or when the pregnancy resulted from rape.

Of course, none of this meant it was simple to get an abortion in Georgia. A woman who met one of the exceptions still needed a doctor to put in writing that, in his or her best medical judgment, the abortion was justified for one of the specified reasons. In addition, two other state-licensed physicians had to concur with this opinion after conducting separate examinations of the woman, the abortion had to be performed in a certified hospital, and an abortion committee of at least three members of the hospital staff had to approve the procedure in advance.

The *Doe v. Bolton* attorneys were claiming that even Georgia's "gentle" approach to abortion regulation was unconstitutional because, no less than Texas's "harsh" approach, it interfered with a woman's right to decide for herself whether to continue or to end a pregnancy. The Court's decision to hear both *Roe* and *Doe* promised the answers to some big questions. A ruling that both Georgia and Texas had violated the "higher law" would mean that the Constitution protected a pure strain of privacy; that a state simply had nothing to say about *why* a woman could legitimately seek an abortion.

During the months they had awaited this news from the Supreme Court, the Weddingtons had left Austin for Fort Worth where Ron took a job with a small firm and Sarah was hired to be an assistant city attorney. She had worked happily in her new position, carrying on her abortion rights efforts on the side. But when the Supreme Court announced it would hear *Roe v. Wade*, Sarah's boss drew the line. He called her into his office. After a short chat, he scrawled a few words on a yellow legal pad, tore off the page, and handed it to her across his desk. It said: "No more women's lib. No more abortion."[2] Sarah was crestfallen. She did not want to abandon the crusade she had begun. After talking it over with Ron, she decided to leave her job with the city and continue her work on the case.

The summer of 1971 found Sarah Weddington encamped in one tiny room of a worn down New York City brownstone, the guest of the James Madison Constitutional Law Institute, an organization that specialized in abortion cases. Roy Lucas, a young attorney, had telephoned to offer the institute's assistance with the *Roe v. Wade* appeal shortly after the Texas panel handed down its decision, and Weddington and Coffee had gratefully accepted. Linda was swamped with work at her job, so Sarah had assumed chief responsibility for pulling together the appeal. She had taken Lucas's offer of help to mean that her own research and writing load would be lightened. Instead, day after day, Sarah found herself in the institute's opulent but chaotic office, not only doing research for her own Supreme Court brief but also typing legal papers to file in the myriad other abortion cases the institute was litigating. When she realized the deadline for filing the *Roe* brief was approaching faster than she was progressing, she asked Ron to come to New York to help her research and write.

With little grumbling, he acceded, came east, and took up residence in her cramped, sweltering quarters. Every day found Ron and Sarah working tirelessly in the tasteful surroundings of the institute. They hammered out every argument they thought the Court might find persuasive: that the medical community overwhelmingly favored legalizing abortion, that the nineteenth-century prohibitions on abortion stemmed from obsolete concerns about protecting women's health, and that the Texas abortion law and others like it violated rights to familial and medical privacy protected by the Constitution. By long distance, they conscripted friends back in Austin to research other historical and legal points at the UT libraries. Glen Wilkerson, a law student Sarah had met through John Sutton, worked on a section of the brief showing that there was no legal precedent for treating the fetus as a person with constitutional rights. In fact, the court decisions that he found suggested just the opposite. He noted, for example, that the U.S. Census Bureau did not count a pregnant woman as two people; that the killing of a pregnant woman was not prosecuted as a double homicide; that a man in Texas who had kicked his pregnant wife until she miscarried was not convicted of murder; and that some states allowed any abortion while others allowed the abortion of fetuses conceived through rape or incest. If the Supreme Court considered the fetus a person, he wrote, none of these decisions could stand.

Ron, Sarah, and the staff at the institute also invested some time looking into the backgrounds of the justices who would hear their case, hoping to craft arguments that would convince them. The only vote they felt sure of winning was that of Justice Douglas, who had written the *Griswold* opinion with its resounding defense of privacy. They hoped it augured well for another vote in their favor when they heard that Justice Stewart's wife was a volunteer at Planned Parenthood. They worried that Justice White would be unsympathetic when it was rumored that he and his wife had had trouble conceiving. It was with Justice Blackmun, the "doctors' lawyer," in mind, that they amassed testimony from the medical community about the hazards of back-alley abortion, the dangers pregnancy posed for certain women, the safety of modern abortion techniques, and the bind in which criminal abortion laws often placed physicians, forcing them to risk arrest and prosecution for acting on their best medical judgment.

The final version of the *Roe* brief came to 145 pages. But the *Roe* attorneys did not leave it at that. They wanted the Supreme Court to understand that large, learned, and credible segments of the American public were on their side. To that end, they solicited additional briefs from dozens of amici curiae (Latin words meaning "friends of the court"). Among the forty "friends" who filed briefs on *Roe*'s behalf were powerful legal, medical, and religious groups including state attorney generals, the American College of Obstetricians and Gynecologists, and the United Methodist church. (On Wade's side, four "friends" filed briefs explaining why they believed abortion should have no place in the Constitution.) The Weddingtons hoped their efforts would convince the Court. Roy Lucas filed the main brief with days to spare before the deadline, and Ron and Sarah returned home to Texas.

Weddington spent the autumn preparing for her oral argument before the High Court. She combed the papers every day for news of the battles for reform or repeal being waged in other states, looking for arguments made in abortion cases in other courts that she might confront or use in the Supreme Court. She convened innumerable "moot courts," sessions where friends and law professors would act as members of the Supreme Court and pepper her with difficult questions about her case. Afterwards, the "justices" would drop their roles, critique her answers to their questions, and discuss how she could have responded better.

Two surprises distracted Sarah from her preparations. First, in the space of six days in September, only weeks before the Court's 1971 term began, two justices, Hugo Black and John Harlan, suddenly resigned because of failing health. Black died a short week later. These unexpected departures increased the likelihood that the Court would postpone argument in the abortion cases until it was fully staffed again with nine justices. They also meant that Richard Nixon, who had denounced abortion on the public record, would have the chance to nominate two new members to the nation's highest court—members who would probably share his convictions about abortion.

Then, in November, just after the Supreme Court

dispelled Weddington's fears by announcing that its seven members would hear argument in *Roe* on December 13, Roy Lucas made contact. The Court had requested the name of the attorney who would argue the case, and Lucas thought it should be his. He sent Sarah a long letter explaining why:

> *It has taken me virtually years to read and absorb everything which might be relevant to the case, and it would be wasteful to not make full use of this experience. As I indicated before, you should be relatively well-prepared on all the issues in the case in the event that I go down in an airplane accident, but every maxim of appellate advocacy demands that the case be presented by one attorney, and that the attorney be the most thoroughly prepared. This is particularly necessary when we know full well that the Doe case is in less than fully capable hands. . . .*
>
> *I trust you will put the best interests of the cause over any personal desires in the matter. . . . It would be a serious mistake to divide the argument [between us], and it is completely out of the question.*[3]

As it turned out, Lucas had already informed the Supreme Court clerk, E. Robert Seaver, that he would be the one to argue *Roe v. Wade.* The Texas plaintiffs bristled at his arrogance. Marsha and David King felt strongly that Weddington should argue their case, and Marsha sent Lucas a telegram saying so. Sarah telephoned Norma McCorvey for the first time in many months to ask whom she would like to represent her before the Supreme Court. Norma remembers Sarah sounding ill at ease on the phone. It took Norma some time to understand that the job "was up for grabs between Sarah and some man in New York."[4] Norma confirmed that Sarah meant some man she had never met, and then she said, "Well, sure. You do it, Sarah." Sarah thanked her and hung up.[5]

To settle the matter, Linda Coffee, as general counsel for the *Roe* plaintiffs, wrote a formal letter to the clerk stating that her clients all wanted Sarah Weddington to present the argument. Within a week, Seaver responded with a letter to Weddington: "In light of the letter I received from Linda N. Coffee dated November 23 . . . , your name is being listed as counsel who will argue for appellants." Having won this battle, Sarah was more anxious than ever. "My stomach is already in knots," she had written to a friend before the conflict was resolved.[6] One of Dr. Hallford's lawyers, Roy Merrill, remembers getting a telephone call from her soon after she heard from Seaver. "I'm going to argue the case," he says Weddington told him, "and then," he reports, "she just broke down crying. I mean, just wept."[7]

Ron and Sarah went to Washington a few days before the hearing was scheduled to get their bearings. Sarah spent a good many hours in the Supreme Court, observing the protocols of oral argument in other cases and studying her notes in the Court library. The newspapers had seized on the novel crusade of two women lawyers fresh out of Texas against the state's century-old criminal abortion law, and when Sarah left the Court library on the day before her argument, a woman working at the desk whispered to her that many Court staffers were rooting for her.[8] Less encouraging, she could not help but notice that the only bathroom in the Supreme Court lawyers' lounge was marked "Men."

The *Roe* argument was scheduled to be heard at ten o'clock on the morning of December 13, with *Doe* to follow immediately. Weddington and Coffee arrived at the Supreme Court with more than an hour to spare. At 9:30, they entered the formal courtroom, an ornate chamber with soaring ceilings painted in deep

Portraits of Supreme Court justices hang in the lawyers' lounge in the Supreme Court Building. While preparing for her oral argument before the Court, Sarah Weddington noted that the only restroom in the lounge was marked "Men."

reds and blues, lined with marble columns. A chastened Roy Lucas eventually took his seat alongside them at the counsel's table near the front of the courtroom. Across the aisle sat the attorneys representing the state of Texas. The room was packed with lawyers, reporters, and spectators. Some had traveled a long way to hear the argument. Amid the crowd were Sarah's mother, Ron, the Kings, Dr. Hallford's attorneys, Roy Merrill and Fred Bruner, and Jane Hodgson, the stalwart Minnesota physician whose criminal conviction would be reversed instantaneously if Sarah Weddington and Margie Hames, the attorney arguing *Doe v. Bolton*, carried the day. Norma McCorvey was not present.

Promptly at ten, the marshal banged his gavel and announced, "The Honorable, the chief justice and the associate justices of the Supreme Court of the United States!" Everyone stood as the heavy velvet curtains behind the bench parted and the black-robed tribunal filed in. After the justices took their seats, another whack of the marshal's gavel signaled that everyone in attendance could be seated as well. From his seat at the center of the bench, Chief Justice Burger announced that the seven-member bench would hear argument in *Roe v. Wade*. Then he said, "Mrs. Weddington, you may proceed whenever you are ready."

Weddington began by explaining why the case was not moot, fending off the argument she anticipated the attorney for Texas would try again. She said Jane Roe had brought suit as soon as she learned she was pregnant, sought an abortion, and was turned away. She underscored the point that the case was a class action. Then she moved into the heart of her argument:

> *In Texas, the woman is the victim. . . . [T]here are problems [with] contraception. Abortion now . . . is safer than childbirth. In the absence of . . . legal, medically safe abortions, women often resort to . . . illegal abortion[s], which . . . carry risks of death, . . . severe infection, permanent sterility . . . or . . . she can do a self-abortion, which is . . . by far the most dangerous. And that is no crime.*[9]

Weddington emphasized that the Texas law made no exceptions if a woman's life was not at risk: "If the pregnancy would result in the birth of a deformed or defective child, she has no relief. Regardless of the circumstances of conception, whether it was because of rape, incest, whether she is extremely immature, she has no relief."[10]
She continued:

Pregnancy to a woman completely disrupts her life. It disrupts her body, it disrupts her education, it disrupts her employment, and it often disrupts her entire family life. And we feel that because of the impact on the woman, this, [if] . . . there are any rights which are fundamental, is of such fundamental and basic concern to the woman involved that she should be allowed to make the choice as to whether to continue or to terminate her pregnancy.[11]

At this point, Justice Stewart interrupted. Weddington had made an eloquent case for showing that the abortion law was bad for society, he told her, but why was it unconstitutional? Weddington had a ready reply. "Your honor," she said, "as I'm sure you're aware," the district court in Texas held that the right to end a pregnancy

rested upon the Ninth Amendment. . . . I do feel that it is . . . an appropriate place for the freedom to rest. I think the Fourteenth Amendment is an equally appropriate place, under the rights of persons to life [and] liberty. I think insofar as liberty is meaningful, that liberty to these women would mean liberty from being forced to continue the unwanted pregnancy.[12]

Stewart pressed further. "You're relying . . . simply on the due process clause of the Fourteenth Amendment?" Weddington told him that originally they had brought the suit claiming the law violated not only the due process clause but the equal protection clause, the Ninth Amendment, "and a variety of others."[13]

"And anything else that might [work]?" Stewart asked, amid laughter. Weddington laughed back, "yeah, right," but she followed with a serious point. "One of the purposes of the Constitution was to guarantee to the individual the right to determine the course of their own lives."[14]

Justice White then posed a troubling question. "Will that take you right up to the time of birth?" Weddington had expected this question and considered her answer carefully. She conceded that she had a difficult time thinking about late-term abortion, but said she believed that the difference between early and late abortion was emotional, not constitutional. White pressed further, asking, emotional for whom? In reply, Weddington made the point her UT law school friend had researched the preceding summer. "I guess by persons considering the issue outside the legal context. The Constitution, as I see it, gives protections to people *after* birth."[15] She cited the cases she had read in which courts had failed to treat a fetus as a person, and by then her thirty minutes were up.

Jay Floyd, the lawyer from the Texas attorney general's office who had fumbled before the three-judge panel in Dallas, rose to make his case. He fumbled again with an ill-chosen opening crack. "Mr. Chief Justice, may it please the Court. It's an old joke, but when a man argues against two beautiful ladies like this, they're going to have the last word."[16] No one laughed. Chief Justice Burger glared.[17]

Floyd shifted his weight from one foot to the other and began his presentation. As Weddington had predicted, he first attacked the plaintiffs' standing, pointing out that Jane Roe was no longer pregnant. The justices of the Supreme Court were no more impressed with this argument than the federal judges in Texas had been. Stewart asked, "What procedure would you suggest for *any* pregnant female in the state of Texas ever to get any judicial consideration of this constitutional claim?"[18] Floyd responded, courageously, in light of the Court's obvious skepticism, that he did not think there was any way a pregnant woman could challenge the law. "I think she makes her choice prior to the time she becomes pregnant. That is the time of the choice," he asserted. Once a child is born, a woman no longer has a choice, and I think pregnancy may terminate that choice. That's when." This prompted a joke from Justice Stewart. "Maybe she makes her choice when she decides to live in Texas." Everyone laughed.[19]

Justice Marshall asked Floyd what interests the state had in regulating abortion that might outweigh a woman's interests in making her own choice. Floyd replied that the state had an interest in protecting fetal life, asserting that "there is life from the moment of impregnation."[20] But when Marshall pressed for scientific data to support the state's claim, Floyd faltered. "Well, we begin, Mr. Justice, in our brief, with the development of the human embryo, carrying it through to the development of the fetus from about seven to nine days after conception."[21]

"Well, what about six days?" Marshall wanted to know.

"We don't know," Floyd was forced to respond.

Marshall showed no mercy. "Well, [but] this statute goes all the way back to one hour."

Finally, Floyd stopped trying. "I don't . . . Mr. Justice there are unanswerable questions in this field!" And finally, he got a laugh.

Marshall relented, to more laughter. "I appreciate it. I appreciate it."[22]

Floyd wrapped up his presentation. Whether to allow abortion, he asserted, is not a question for the courts but for the voters. "There is nothing in the United States Constitution concerning birth, contraception, or abortion," he said. "We think these matters are matters of policy, which should be properly addressed by the state legislature."[23] Weddington made a short rebuttal, and the argument was over. The Court moved on to *Doe v. Bolton.*

Afterwards, Weddington was giddy with relief but she could scarcely remember anything she had said. Riding in a taxi back to the hotel with friends, Ron recounted the argument, grading her performance. To one of her friends, some of his comments sounded a little sarcastic. Everyone convened later that evening for a celebratory dinner, and the next day, after reading the newspaper stories about the case over breakfast, the Weddingtons headed home.

In the wake of their trip to Washington, the culmination of more than a year's work, both Ron and Sarah felt deflated. As Sarah's star was rising, their marriage was sinking. Ron chafed at working behind the scenes of Sarah's triumphs. He had helped her think through every argument she presented in *Roe v. Wade*, and sweated alongside her over the brief through the New York summer. Sarah had gotten all the recognition. The demands on her time were growing. She had less time to spend with Ron, and they had begun to argue.

Sarah found distraction in a new project before any word on *Roe* came down from the Supreme Court. On February 7, 1972, she announced her intention to run for the Texas House of Representatives. Her abortion work had earned her some fame and many supporters. On June 3, she won in the primary elections. Just over three weeks later, the Supreme Court announced without giving a reason that it would hear reargument in both *Roe* and *Doe.* President Nixon had

Ron Weddington helped his wife, Sarah, prepare the brief and oral argument for Roe v. Wade.

appointed two new justices, Lewis Powell and William Rehnquist, to replace Black and Harlan, and the press speculated that the justices had decided it would be best to have a full bench decide the most controversial cases of the term.

Roy Lucas immediately launched a letter to Weddington explaining for the second time why he, and not she, should be the one to argue *Roe* before the Court. He wrote, melodramatically, that being taken off the first argument was

> *like being told: Thank you for getting jurisdiction, and for four years of your life, and for going into debt up to and beyond your ears, but no thanks. It seemed incomprehensible. . . . It takes a lot of experience and dedication to be able to anticipate and respond to the Court's questions in a way which strengthens your case. . . . [M]uch of your argument was well done, but much could have been far better, and that is crucial with a sharply and closely divided Court. . . . Not only do a few Justices appear to be wavering, . . . but also the questioning will be much more difficult and intense.*[24]

Weddington did not take the time from her campaign to reply to Lucas, but she did write and file a seventeen-page supplementary brief with the Supreme Court, citing relevant cases that had been decided since the first argument in December. She included the statistic that during the last nine months of 1971, a total of 1,658 Texas women had gone to New York to seek abortions.[25] She also addressed Floyd's claim from the first hearing that Texas's abortion law had been passed to protect fetal life. "[S]ince self-[induced] abortion is not a crime in Texas, it is not logical to assume that the purpose of the . . . law was to protect the fetus. It is logical that the . . . purpose was to protect the woman and her health."[26] Sarah took only a few days to review her notes and to practice the argument, and at midnight on the eve of her departure for Washington, six or eight people were still in her conference room going over critical points.[27]

When she entered the formal courtroom to argue her case for the second time on October 11, 1972, Sarah knew better what to expect. This time, Ron sat with her and Linda at the counsel's table, and Roy Lucas took a seat in the lawyers' section. This time, Weddington managed to talk for almost ten minutes before anyone from the panel interrupted her. She restated what she asserted were the constitutional bases for the right to abortion, citing the "great body of cases [the Court had already] decided . . . [relating to] marriage, sex, contraception, procreation, childbearing, and education of children, which say there are certain things that are so much a part of the individual concern that they should be left to the determination of the individual."[28] She also mentioned that the maternal death rate in New York had decreased by two-thirds to a record low after that state repealed its abortion restrictions in 1971.

Justice White demanded to know if it was critical to Weddington's case that the Fourteenth Amendment did not protect the fetus. She answered that, if the fetus were considered a person, then a state would have a legitimate interest in protecting its life. But, she argued, the state would still have to balance that interest against the woman's interest in her own liberty. White was not satisfied. "If it were established that an unborn fetus is a person, within the protection of the Fourteenth Amendment, you would have an almost impossible case here, would you not?" he asked. Weddington conceded, "I would have a *very* difficult case."[29]

Justice Blackmun raised the question that had seemed to trouble the Court at the first hearing. "Do you make any distinction between the first and ninth month of gestation?"[30] Weddington parried, saying the state of Texas made no such distinction. Then Justice Brennan asked if she thought the Court would contradict its recent ruling outlawing the death penalty if it accepted her argument that abortion should be allowed at the other end of the life span. Weddington said she did not think it would be inconsistent if the Constitution were interpreted to allow abortion but to prohibit capital punishment because the fetus, unlike the condemned criminal, had never been recognized as a person.

Texas had not sent Jay Floyd back to Washington for a second round. Instead, this time, Robert Flowers, Floyd's boss, stood to defend the state's law. As Weddington had focused her second argument more closely on the constitutional principles protecting a woman's right to choose abortion, Flowers had focused his on the state's interest in preventing abortion. He declared, "It is the position of the state of Texas that upon conception we have a human being, a person within the concept of the Constitution."[31]

The justices, too, had honed in since the first hearing on the central issue of the case: whether the fetus was a person having the same constitutional status as its mother. They pounced immediately on Flowers's statement. Wasn't a legislature out of its depth answering the question of when human life begins? Justice Stewart asked, "Is it a legal question, a constitutional question, a medical question . . . what is it?"[32] The assistant attorney general flailed, answering that a legislature could best answer the question because it could hear medical testimony on the subject. "Then it's basically a medical decision?" Stewart asked.[33]

"From a constitutional standpoint, no sir," Flowers responded. "I think it's fairly and squarely before this Court. We don't envy the Court for having to make this decision."[34] The Court pressed for any clear

The members of the Supreme Court who heard the October 1972 reargument of Roe v. Wade *posed for this photo in April 1972. Reargument of the case allowed newly appointed justices William Rehnquist (standing, far right) and Lewis Powell (standing, far left) to participate in the decision.*

authority Flowers could point to saying the fetus was a person. Was there any case? Stewart wanted to know. Flowers knew of none. Instead, he tried to invoke the views of William Blackstone, the revered eighteenth-century English legal commentator. Justice Blackmun interrupted, but wasn't it "true that in Blackstone's time abortion was not a felony?"[35]

Flowers had to concede that Blackmun was correct. Having lost his footing in Blackstone, he tried to ground his stance in the opinions of the men who wrote the Constitution, but Justice Stewart reminded him that the Fourteenth Amendment, protecting "persons," was ratified almost three-quarters of a century after the framers were dead. Blackmun pressed him to acknowledge that there was no consensus even among doctors "as to when life begins."[36]

Flowers was finally allowed to return to his original point, that, in Texas, anyway, the fetus was a person "within the framework of the U.S. Constitution and the Texas Constitution."[37] Stewart responded, "Of course, if you're right about that, you can sit down. You've won your case."[38] Flowers heartily agreed, but Justice White raised the corresponding point: "You think the case is over for you? You've lost your case, then, if the fetus or embryo is not a person; is that it?"[39] Again, Flowers agreed. But he urged the Court to remember its antimajoritarian function:

> *This Court has not been blind to the rights of the unborn child in the past . . . . [The] Court has been diligent in protecting the rights of the minority. And gentlemen, we say that this is a minority, a silent minority, the true silent minority. Who is speaking for these children? Where is the counsel for these unborn children, whose life is being taken? Where is the safeguard of the right to trial by jury?*[40]

Justice Stewart interrupted to say that if Flowers was right that the fetus was a person, then, if anything, Texas's law might be *too* permissive because it allowed abortion in some cases. In fact, he added, it would be grossly unconstitutional to let any legislature decide to allow the killing of some persons. Justice Rehnquist pressed the issue, asking if the exceptions some states made for rape and incest didn't "indicate that the weight of history [wa]s against the concept of life from the moment of conception."[41] The justices' point was a subtle one: if it is the sanctity of life—as opposed to the chastity of women—that abortion laws were intended to protect, then how could we justify ending *some* pregnancies—those resulting from women's victimization—and not others? Aren't all fetuses created equal?

Flowers closed his presentation by saying, "I think that here is exactly what we're facing in this case: Is the life of this unborn fetus paramount over the woman's right to determine whether or not she shall bear a child? . . . Are we to place th[e] power [to decide] in the hands of a mother, in a doctor?"[42]

Weddington stood to give her rebuttal:

No one is more keenly aware of the gravity of the issues or the moral implications of this case. But it is a case that must be decided on the Constitution. We do not disagree that there is a progression of fetal development. It is the conclusion to be drawn from that upon which we disagree. We are not here to advocate abortion. We do not ask this Court to rule that abortion is good or desirable in any particular situation. We are here to advocate that the decision as to whether or not a particular woman will continue to carry or will terminate a pregnancy is a decision that should be made by that individual. That in fact she has a constitutional right to make that decision for herself, and that the state has shown no interest in interfering with that decision.[43]

She had the clear impression as she left the courtroom that the justices had already made up their minds.

Chapter 8
VICTORY

Less than a month after her second argument in the Supreme Court, Sarah Weddington was elected to the Texas House of Representatives. She immediately set about drafting a bill to repeal the state abortion law that she would propose on the legislative floor in the event that bad news came down from the Supreme Court. She was sworn in on January 9, 1973. Ten days later, she filed her first legislative package, which included the repeal bill, another one authorizing females aged sixteen and older to consent to abortion, and a third allowing doctors to give contraceptives to women under eighteen without notice to their parents.[1]

Richard Nixon was inaugurated to his second term as president on January 20. Sarah and Ron, who had drifted farther apart since her campaign, watched miserably on television. Another rumor about why the Supreme Court had insisted on hearing reargument in the abortion cases was that Nixon had not wanted the decisions announced during his run for reelection.

Weddington left early for the state capitol on the following Monday. A reporter from the *New York Times* called her home office shortly after nine o'clock, asking if Mrs. Weddington had any comment on *Roe v. Wade*. When Sarah's assistant asked if there was any special reason why she should, the reporter told her the decision had been announced in Washington that

*Sarah Weddington is sworn in as a member of the
Texas House of Representatives on January 9, 1973.*

morning. "She won," he said.[2] By a vote of seven to
two, the Supreme Court had invalidated both the
Texas and the Georgia abortion laws. Within five minutes, the phones were ringing off the hook.

It wasn't until a few days later that Weddington
actually received a copy of the full Supreme Court
opinion in the mail. She had read long quotations from
it in the press, but she was awed and gratified when

she finally held it in her hands and confirmed for herself the true sweep of the ruling. She shivered to read Justice Blackmun's words in the majority opinion:

> *We forthwith acknowledge our awareness of the sensitive and emotional nature of the abortion controversy, of the vigorous opposing views, even among physicians, and of the deep and seemingly absolute convictions that the subject inspires. One's philosophy, one's experiences, one's exposure to the raw edges of human existence, one's religious training, one's attitudes toward life and family and their values, and the moral standards one establishes and seeks to observe, are all likely to influence and to color one's thinking and conclusions about abortion.*[3]

First, the Court announced, Jane Roe had standing to initiate the action. That she had given birth more than a year before the Supreme Court ever heard of her did not render the case moot. To deny her a hearing on that ground, as the state of Texas had urged, would be to place formality over reality because no normal pregnancy outlasted the life of a typical federal case. The Court refused to create such a class of cases that, by their very nature, would be "capable of repetition, yet evading review."[4]

In contrast, the Court denied standing to both Dr. Hallford and the Kings. Dr. Hallford, it was noted, had another avenue of relief in that he could raise his claim in the state court that would hold his criminal trial, and the injury the Kings alleged they suffered because of the Texas abortion law was too remote to afford them standing.

The body of the opinion appeared to reflect hundreds of hours of historical research. (In 1992, Blackmun would tell a reporter from the *Washington Post* that he had spent two full weeks in the medical library of the Mayo Clinic gathering facts for the *Roe* opinion.[5]) First, Blackmun pointed out that the criminal abortion laws most Americans lived under were of "relatively recent vintage."[6] He went on to discuss the generally permissive attitudes toward abortion of the ancient Greeks and Romans and the views reflected in the Hippocratic oath taken by doctors, the unwritten "common" law that preceded American and English criminal codes, and Christian theology. Finally, he described the formal positions that the American Medical Association, the American Public Health Association, and the American Bar Association had taken on abortion.

Next, he wrote about a state's possible interests in restricting abortion. He dismissed with little fuss the position of some commentators that criminal abortion laws were passed to discourage illicit sexual conduct. Then, he moved on to a more substantial justification: the state's interest in abortion as a medical procedure. What appeared to be the laws' original purpose—to protect women from the risks of surgery before the advent of antibiotics—he noted, was now obsolete. The state still had an important interest, however, in seeing to it that only qualified practitioners performed abortions, and only in properly equipped facilities.

Last, Blackmun discussed Texas's asserted interest in protecting fetal life. For a state to have a valid interest, he wrote, it was not necessary that human life begin at conception. At some point in pregnancy, he maintained, the state could rightly assert an interest in *potential* life, and restrict abortion in the name of that interest. But until that point, he wrote, getting to the heart of the case, *a woman's own liberty outweighed the state's interest in her fetus.*

He described the constitutional right to privacy as a species of liberty, which a state that prohibited abortion in early pregnancy infringed:

101

*The Constitution does not explicitly mention
any right of privacy. In a line of decisions, however, going back perhaps as far as . . . 1891, the
Court has recognized that a right of personal
privacy . . . does exist under the Constitution. In
varying contexts, the Court or individual
Justices have . . . found at least the roots of that
right in the First Amendment, . . . in the Fourth
and Fifth Amendments, . . . in the Ninth
Amendment, . . . or in the concept of liberty
guaranteed by the first section of the
Fourteenth Amendment. These decisions make
it clear that only personal rights that can be
deemed "fundamental" . . . are included in this
guarantee of personal privacy. They also make
it clear that the right has some extension to
activities relating to marriage, . . . procreation,
. . . contraception, . . . family relationships, . . .
and child rearing and education.*

*This right of privacy, whether it be founded
in the Fourteenth Amendment's concept of personal liberty . . . , as we feel it is, or, as the District
Court determined, in the Ninth Amendment's
reservation of rights to the people, is broad
enough to encompass a woman's decision
whether or not to terminate her pregnancy.*[7]

And he wrote about the heavy personal burdens of
pregnancy, which a state that prohibited abortion
forced an unwilling woman to carry:

*The detriment that the State would impose
upon the pregnant woman by denying this
choice altogether is apparent. Specific and
direct harm medically diagnosable even in
early pregnancy may be involved. Maternity, or
additional offspring, may force upon the*

*woman a distressful life and future.
Psychological harm may be imminent. Mental
and physical health may be taxed by child care.
There is also the distress, for all concerned,
associated with the unwanted child, and there
is the problem of bringing a child into a family
already unable, psychologically and otherwise,
to care for it. In other cases, as in this one, the
additional difficulties and continuing stigma
of unwed motherhood may be involved.*[8]

Nobody knows when human life begins, Blackmun wrote. And the Supreme Court would not guess:

*When those trained in the respective disciplines
of medicine, philosophy, and theology are
unable to arrive at any consensus, the judiciary,
at this point in the development of man's
knowledge, is not in a position to speculate as
to the answer.*

*It should be sufficient to note . . . the wide
divergence of thinking on this most sensitive
and difficult question.*[9]

The law had never treated the unborn "as persons in the whole sense," he wrote, citing the myriad cases Weddington's research had unearthed on that point.

"In view of all this," he concluded, "we do not agree that, by adopting one theory of life, Texas may override the rights of the pregnant woman that are at stake."[10] Striking a careful balance between the woman's rights and a state's interests, *Roe* established a constitutional calculus based on the three "trimesters" of pregnancy. At any time during the first three months, or trimester, a woman can get an abortion for any or no reason without interference from the state. After the first trimester, when abortion is slightly riskier, a state may regulate the procedure to protect the woman's health. Throughout the third trimester, when the fetus is "viable," or capable of living outside the womb, the state's interest in potential life becomes compelling enough that the state can prohibit abortion altogether unless it will endanger a woman's life or health to carry a child to term. Weddington was not a little surprised at this seeming attempt at a diplomatic resolution of the constitutional dispute between Roe and Wade. No one on either side had ever said anything about dividing the pregnancy into trimesters.

Chief Justice Burger and Justices Douglas and Stewart wrote separate opinions concurring with the majority. Justice Douglas eloquently described the rights unmentioned by the Constitution as those "that come within the sweep of 'the Blessings of Liberty'" mentioned in the preamble.[11] He canvassed the Court's earlier decisions protecting familial privacy, including *Meyer, Pierce, Skinner,* and *Griswold.* And he recounted the famous language the Court had used a year earlier to explain how the Constitution sheltered the right to use birth control: "If the right of privacy means anything, it is the right of the *individual,* married or single, to be free from unwarranted governmental intrusion into matters so fundamentally affecting a person as the decision whether to bear or beget a child."[12] The criminal prohibitions on abortion, he wrote, were "at war with the clear message of these cases—that a woman is free to make the basic decision whether to bear an unwanted child."[13]

Justices White and Rehnquist each dissented. Justice Rehnquist questioned whether the case should have been dismissed as moot because it wasn't even certain that Jane Roe had been in her first trimester at the time she filed suit. He made it clear, though, that he heartily disagreed with his colleagues on the merits of the case as well. Justice

White saw no justification in the Constitution for thwarting the will of a majority of voters as it was expressed in the criminal abortion statutes. He wrote fierce words, in which Rehnquist joined:

> *I find nothing in the language or history of the Constitution to support the Court's judgment. The Court simply fashions and announces a new constitutional right for pregnant mothers and, with scarcely any reason or authority for its action, invests that right with sufficient substance to override most existing state abortion statutes. The upshot is that the people and the legislatures of the 50 States are constitutionally disentitled to weigh the relative importance of the continued existence and development of the fetus, on the one hand, against a spectrum of possible impacts on the mother, on the other hand. . . .*
>
> *The Court apparently values the convenience of the pregnant mother more than the continued existence and development of the life or potential life that she carries. Whether or not I agree with that marshaling of values, I can in no event join the Court's judgment because I find no constitutional warrant for imposing such an order of priorities on the people and legislatures of the States. In a sensitive area such as this, involving as it does issues over which reasonable men may easily and heatedly differ, I cannot accept the Court's exercise of its clear power of choice by interposing a constitutional barrier to state efforts to protect human life and by investing mothers and doctors with the constitutionally protected right to exterminate it.*[14]

Overnight, *Roe v. Wade* eliminated criminal prohibitions on abortion in forty-four states. *Doe v. Bolton* simultaneously abolished the requirement in some states that abortions be performed in hospitals. The unidentified Texas woman whose predicament had enabled Sarah and Linda to state a claim in federal court read about the decisions in the morning papers.

One good thing had finally happened to Norma McCorvey. In 1970, a few months after she awoke from her suicide attempt, she found herself jobless and hungry. She wandered into a corner store on the edge of a Mexican neighborhood, thinking to steal something to eat. The manager, a woman, was talking on the telephone with her back to the door as McCorvey entered. It looked like an easy crime. McCorvey roamed through the aisles, stuffing a box of crackers, a can of soup, and two Cokes under her blouse. A breeze. She was halfway out the door when she heard the manager behind her. "You know, I really should call the cops on you."[15] When Norma turned around, the woman was smiling at her. A month later, Norma agreed to live with her.

When Connie Gonzales came to pick up Norma's belongings and bring her to the house where she now has lived for almost twenty years, she took Norma's father outside and spoke to him privately. She promised him that she would take care of Norma for the rest of her life and that she would never knowingly let anyone else hurt her. "And whatever has happened . . . since then," Norma writes, "she has never broken her promise."[16]

McCorvey and Gonzales launched a business together, cleaning and painting commercial apartment buildings. It was hard, dirty work. Every morning, they left the house at five, loaded down with mops, brooms, rags, Comet, and Lysol. Every evening, they returned worn out, their hands chapped and grimy, and their coveralls caked with paint and filth. The proceeds from their new enterprise helped pay for home delivery of the *Dallas Times-Herald*.

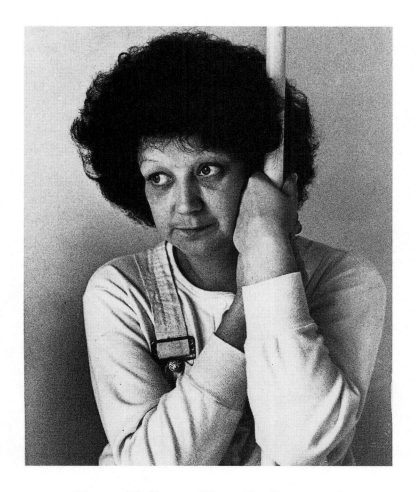

*Norma McCorvey ("Jane Roe"), pictured
here in 1983, never had an abortion.*

At the end of one long day in early 1973, while
Connie showered off the residue of fourteen hours'
work, Norma sat at the kitchen table, drinking a beer
and scanning the front page. "There was a small, mat-
ter-of-fact article that said that the United States
Supreme Court had legalized abortion all over the
United States."[17] Norma's breathing slowed as she read.

Connie, wet-haired and dressed in clean clothes, found Norma sitting in the kitchen, looking into space. "What's wrong, honey?" she asked.

"They've legalized abortion," Norma told her, showing her the article.

"Oh. Okay. That's good," Connie replied, reading.

After a minute, Norma interrupted her. "Connie. Do you see where they mention the plaintiff? A woman called Jane Roe?"

"Yeah. Sure I do," said Connie, looking puzzled.

Norma looked straight at her and said, "How would you like to meet Jane Roe?"

Connie frowned a little and laughed. "Oh, Pixie, come on," she said. "We don't know anybody like that."[18]

Chapter 9
BACKLASH

Although many people greeted the *Roe* decision with shouts of joy, others found the ruling absolutely shocking. One woman remembers that she was frosting a cake for her son's third birthday when her husband showed her the article in a newspaper.

> *And I read that and it very much upset me. I've got that paper to this day. . . . And I sat down, I was very upset. . . . I wanted to cry in a way. . . . All of these things in my personal life—things that were no concern of mine, so to speak, you say "that's somebody else's business"—all came together in one. And being Jamie's birthday, my very first son . . . that kind of made it a personal thing . . . almost like seeing Providence. God was saying, "Lookit, sister, you better see what's going on there."*[1]

Another says that she and her friends "felt as though the bottom had been pulled out from under us. It was an incredible thing, I couldn't believe it. In fact, I didn't. For a couple of months I kept thinking, 'It can't be right, I'm not hearing what I'm hearing.'"[2]

Roe v. Wade stunned thousands of quiet citizens who had believed their whole lives that abortion was murder. More than an opinion, it was something they *knew*; it was self-evident. They were deeply troubled that the highest court in the land would deny anything so obvious, would say, "it's too murky and too personal for a legislature to decide." Who, if not police, district attorneys, and judges, would protect the unborn? There was a higher law, they believed, *the word of God*, and if the government would not enforce it, then the *faithful* would have to. Many people report that they became mobilized to the pro-life cause on the very day *Roe* was handed down.[3] The Supreme Court's once-and-for-all decision brought legion opponents of legal abortion out of the woodwork.

In her book, *Abortion and the Politics of Motherhood* (1984), sociologist Kristin Luker compares the women who became pro-life activists in the wake of *Roe v. Wade* with those who worked to make and keep abortion legal. The average pro-life woman, she reports, married at seventeen, has three or more children, has some college education, does not work in the paid labor force, has an annual family income of $30,000, is Catholic, and attends church at least once a week. In contrast, the average pro-choice woman married at twenty-two, has one or two children, has some graduate or professional training beyond college, has a regular job and an annual family income of more than $50,000, feels that religion is not important to her, and attends church very rarely, if at all.[4] Luker observes that, for vastly more pro-life than pro-choice women, motherhood is a way of life.

To many foes of abortion, social activism came naturally. Founded on the sturdy pillars of family, church, and community, the Right to Life movement is perhaps the best-organized American political force this century has seen. The message that human life is sacred from the moment of conception is broadcast from the pulpits and over the airwaves to a dedicated audience that is already bound by a common religious

Participants in a 1985 March for Life in Washington, D.C., protest the Supreme Court's decision in Roe v. Wade.

world view. Weekly church services provide the opportunity for pro-life activists to meet, sign petitions, write letters, and plan concerted activity.

The day *Roe* was decided, a day opponents of the ruling call "Black Monday," having reproductive freedom read back *out* of the Constitution became the top priority of the newly inspired antiabortion movement. The Right to Life movement attacked *Roe* on many fronts: in the legislatures, in the courts, and in the media. Money and energy poured into the campaigns of politicians who believed the *Roe* decision should be undone. State legislatures and the U.S. Congress set to work writing laws that would test the constitutional limits of pregnant women's newly announced right to privacy. Frustrated that they could no longer prohibit abortions altogether, lawmakers came up with dozens of ways to make them hard to get. And in time, the federal courts, staffed with many new judges picked between 1981 and 1992 by two avowedly pro-life presidents, Reagan and Bush, began to uphold these measures that bent, without quite breaking, the "higher law" *Roe* had announced.

Before the eighties had dawned, *Roe*'s opponents began to see results from their efforts. Just four years after the decision was issued, Congress passed the Hyde Amendment, a law preventing the use of Medicaid funds to pay for poor women's abortions. Medicaid, a federal program meant to provide medical care for low income families, still pays for poor women to carry their pregnancies to term. The restriction was not passed as an economy measure; Congress recognized that the costs a woman incurs in childbearing and child-rearing far exceed the cost of an abortion. And Congress is well aware that when a pregnant woman is on welfare, the taxpayers bear these costs, however grudgingly. The Hyde Amendment simply reflects Congress's *moral* judgment that pregnant women should have children, not abortions.

In 1980, *Harris v. McRae*,[5] a class action filed on behalf of indigent women, challenged the Hyde Amendment, claiming that it violated the Constitution by restricting poor women's freedom to choose whether to terminate their pregnanies. The Supreme Court, in a five-to-four vote, disagreed. The majority reasoned that while *Roe* prohibited the government from "placing obstacles in the path" of a woman's exercise of her right to abortion, it did not oblige the government to remove obstacles, like poverty, that were not of its own creation. Funding childbirth but not abortion, the Court ruled, was a permissible way for the government to express its opinion that it was "in the public interest" for poor women to have children, whether they wanted them or not.

Justice Brennan wrote an incisive dissent. "By funding all of the expenses associated with childbirth and none of the expenses incurred in terminating the pregnancy, the government literally makes an offer that the indigent woman cannot afford to refuse." Studies show that Justice Brennan was right: the Hyde Amendment has "persuaded" significant numbers of Medicaid-eligible women who want abortions to have children instead.[6]

In 1986, with Ronald Reagan comfortably settled in the White House, the Missouri Catholic Conference and local right-to-life groups joined forces to pass a law they hoped would give Reagan's Supreme Court appointees a chance to overturn *Roe*. The law barred abortion in public hospitals and forbade public employees to perform an abortion or counsel a woman to seek an abortion that was not necessary to save her life. A group of doctors and patients sued William Webster, the state attorney general, claiming the law was unconstitutional. The federal appeals court in St. Louis agreed and struck down the statute on the ground that it conflicted with the Supreme Court's ruling in *Roe v. Wade*.

In 1989, when the case known as *Webster v. Reproductive Health Services*[7] finally made its way to the Supreme Court, Justices Scalia and Kennedy— President Reagan's picks—had replaced Burger and Powell, and Rehnquist, who had dissented in *Roe*, was the new chief justice. This newly composed Supreme Court said the appeals court had misread *Roe* and reinstated the Missouri law.

The *Webster* decision, in many ways, was the logical extension of *McRae*'s holding that the government could express its disapproval of abortion by refusing to have anything to do with it. The five-member majority wrote, "nothing in the Constitution requires States to enter or remain in the abortion business." Equally troubling to those who had worked to make *Roe* the law of the land, the Court left untouched the Missouri law's preamble, which declares that "the life of each human being begins at conception" and "unborn children have protectable interests in life, health and well being." Justice Blackmun, dissenting, accused his colleagues of "implicitly invit[ing] every state legislature to enact more and more restrictive regulations."

In 1981, some years before Missouri went to the legislative drawing board to limit poor women's access to abortion, Minnesota had passed the most restrictive minors' abortion law in the country. The statute, drawn up by the state's leading pro-life group, requires a young woman's doctor to notify both of her biological parents personally or by certified mail at least 48 hours before performing an abortion. The law applies to all women under the age of eighteen, including married minors, minors who already have children, minors from broken homes, and minors pregnant through incest. The law applies even if the minor's biological parents are divorced or were never married. (An early version of the bill would also have required notice to the fetus's paternal grandparents.)

A Minnesota minor who wants to avoid notifying her parents has to prove to a judge that she is mature enough to choose abortion for herself or that it would not serve her best interests for her parents to know. Since one-parent notification is not adequate in Minnesota, the law often requires a mother to go into court with her daughter to ask permission not to tell the minor's father about the abortion decision.

With *Webster* already in the pipeline, Dr. Jane Hodgson, in her seventies and still a champion of legal abortion, challenged the Minnesota statute in federal court. The legal question was whether the state's interest in two-parent notification outweighed a minor's interest in privacy. Minnesota argued that the statute promoted family unity: "in the ideal family, the minor should make her decision only after consultation with both parents who should naturally be concerned with the child's welfare." The trial court noted one additional purpose of the law: "influential supporters of the measure hoped it 'would save lives' by influencing minors to carry their pregnancies to term rather than aborting."

Because teenage women in Minnesota had been living under the law for years before Dr. Hodgson filed suit, there was abundant evidence from which the trial court could see how the law actually worked. In a five-week-long trial, the plaintiffs presented the testimony of counselors, psychologists, juvenile court judges, physicians, state attorneys, and dozens of young women. Judges who heard minors' abortion petitions unanimously opposed the procedure, testifying that: minors found it "a very nerve-racking experience"; "going to court [i]s absolutely traumatic for minors . . . at a very, very difficult time in their lives." One judge stated, "I do not see anything that is being accomplished that is useful to anybody." Dr. Hodgson testified that when her minor patients return from court, "some of them are wringing wet with perspiration. They're markedly relieved. They . . . dread the court procedure often more than the actual abortion procedure, and . . . it's frequently necessary to give them a sedative of some kind beforehand."

After hearing testimony like this, the trial court struck down the law, observing that it had little impact on "ideal families," in which minor daughters voluntarily confided in their parents. In contrast, the court found, the statute's burdens landed heaviest on young women whose families fell short of the "ideal"—the fifty percent of minors in Minnesota who did not live with both of their biological parents. The evidence showed that the law did not resurrect communication between a minor and an absent parent and that forced notification of an abusive parent often provoked violence.

The Supreme Court upheld the law in 1990, despite this powerful trial record. A majority in *Hodgson v. Minnesota*[8] wrote that, although it was "clear that the requirement that both parents be notified, whether or not both wished to be notified or have assumed responsibility for the upbringing of the child, does not reasonably further any legitimate state interest," the statute was constitutional because the minor could avoid notifying one or both parents by going to court.

It was left for the "three old goats"—as Justice Blackmun called himself, Brennan, and Marshall, who were all past eighty—to dissent. The trial record, they pointed out, was full of "examples of parents who were drunk and abusive and who beat and intimidated their children, [as well as] teenagers [who] got pregnant in hopes of escaping an unhappy home."[9] Blackmun wrote that he found it "bewildering" that the majority showed a "selective blindness to this stark social reality." Marshall said these state laws "force a young woman in an already dire situation to choose between two fundamentally unacceptable alternatives: notifying a possibly dictatorial or even abusive parent or justifying her profoundly personal decision in an intimidating judicial proceeding to a black-robed stranger." *Hodgson* and its companion case, *Ohio v. Akron Center for Reproductive Health*, "cleared the way for at least thirty-one states to enforce laws restricting the abortion rights of teenagers."[10]

One year after *Hodgson* was decided, with Justice

Brennan retired, the Court upheld a Health and Human Services Administration regulation that prevented employees of federally funded family planning clinics from telling their patients—mostly poor women and teenagers—that abortion is legal and available. Under this "gag rule," clinics that accept federal money (known as Title X funds) have to refer every pregnant client "for appropriate prenatal . . . services" by giving her a list of agencies that "promote the welfare of the mother and the unborn child." A Title X clinic may not refer a pregnant woman to an abortion provider even if she asks. The Court's majority wrote, "It would undoubtedly be easier for a woman seeking an abortion if she could receive information about abortion from a Title X project, but the Constitution does not require that the Government . . . provide that information."

Before *Rust v. Sullivan*,[11] the Title X case, the Court had upheld laws that limited women's *access* to abortion, but it had never allowed a law that limited access to *information* about abortion. Three justices argued that the Title X regulation, by restricting speech, violated the First Amendment as well as the right to privacy. Justice Blackmun wrote in dissent, "Until today, the Court has allowed to stand only those restrictions upon reproductive freedom that, while limiting the availability of abortion, have left intact a woman's ability to decide without coercion whether she will continue her pregnancy to term. Today's decision abandons that principle, and with disastrous results. . . . Both the purpose and result of the challenged regulation is to deny women the ability voluntarily to decide their procreative destiny."

In one of his first official actions as president, Bill Clinton lifted the Title X gag rule in 1993 on the twentieth anniversary of *Roe v. Wade*. The Supreme Court's decision in *Rust* still stands, however, inviting any president who is less kindly disposed toward abortion to reinstate the rule.

✳ Most recently, in 1992, the Court upheld the Pennsylvania Abortion Control Act in *Planned Parenthood of Southeastern Pennsylvania v. Casey*. The Act requires a woman to give her informed consent to the abortion procedure and to wait twenty-four hours after consenting before getting an abortion. Under the law, a woman's consent is not "informed" until a physician tells her that, if she decides to bear the child, she may qualify for state medical assistance and the father will be liable for child support payments. In addition, the physician has to offer her information generated by the state describing and picturing the fetus in various stages from fertilization through nine months' gestation and provide a list of agencies offering alternatives to abortion. Physicians who fail to "counsel" their patients according to the law risk criminal prosecution.

The Supreme Court upheld these requirements even though the record showed that state benefits were usually insufficient to support a child and that, in 1988, only one-quarter of child support payment orders issued by Pennsylvania courts were actually enforced. The Court regarded the twenty-four-hour mandatory delay as reasonable to ensure that women made their choices carefully. In fact, because abortion providers are few and far between in Pennsylvania, the twenty-four hours the law requires usually stretches into a wait of forty-eight hours to two weeks, pushing women later into pregnancy. Women who travel hundreds of miles to obtain abortions pay the added costs of transportation, overnight lodging, lost wages, food, and childcare. And, by forcing women to make two visits to the clinic, the law exposes them twice to the possible harassment of antiabortion protesters.

At the oral argument of *Casey*, Pennsylvania's

lawyers predictably urged the Supreme Court to overrule *Roe v. Wade*. Not so predictable was the appearance of lawyers representing the *United States*, sent by pro-life president George Bush to urge the same. The Court, invoking the tradition of stare decisis, refused to jettison its prior decision. States would not be allowed to criminalize abortion again.

Still, the *Casey* opinion left many people confused. The Supreme Court claimed that it was standing behind *Roe v. Wade*. But in the same breath, the Court *affirmed* the decision of the lower court, which had pronounced *Roe* dead! The Supreme Court explained that in a few cases it decided after *Roe*, it had interpreted the right to choose too broadly and given women seeking abortions too much freedom from state interference. *Casey* "corrected" this trend by softening the constitutional test to which abortion laws had traditionally been subjected. After *Casey*, a state no longer has to show that an abortion law is necessary to serve a compelling interest. Now, it must show only that the restriction does not "unduly burden" a woman's freedom to choose.

The Supreme Court has yet to say exactly how heavy an "undue" burden is, but measured against this new standard, many of the laws that were once struck down under *Roe* are now considered constitutional. Chief Justice Rehnquist put it like this: "*Roe* continues to exist, but only in the way a storefront on a western movie set exists: a mere facade to give the illusion of reality." Sarah Weddington, who visited the Supreme Court in 1992 to hear the oral argument in *Casey*, noticed that the only bathroom was still marked "Men."[12]

Today, Rehnquist's sardonic comment rings true to many pro-choice activists: the Court's decisions have placed the right *Roe* announced beyond the reach of thousands of poor and young women. But to many

Celebrities lead a 1992 pro-choice march in Washington, D.C., to protest the erosion of abortion rights.

pro-life activists, these victories are overshadowed by the bitter fact that abortion *is*, and under the Constitution it *must remain*, legal in every state.

Casey had taken the Supreme Court to the brink of turning back history. When five justices in that decision declined the invitation of Pennsylvania and the president to overrule *Roe* outright, defenders of legal abortion breathed a shaky sigh of relief. A small but lethal faction of the pro-life movement sprang to arms. If they could not make abortion illegal, they vowed to make it impossible.

Five years before *Casey*, Randall Terry, a used-car salesman from upstate New York, founded Operation Rescue (OR), an organization whose mission was to block women from entering abortion clinics. As Terry explained upon launching OR, "There is no difference between killing a four-year-old child and aborting a pre-born three-month-old." His pastor, the Reverend Daniel J. Little, concludes that *Roe v. Wade* "legalized murder, [so there is] very little choice of what you are supposed to do. It is no longer a matter of choice, it is a matter of conviction."[13]

Operation Rescue volunteers have thronged abortion clinics since the late eighties, praying, chanting, shouting, displaying enormous photographs of stillborn infants, and pitching tiny plastic fetuses at women entering the clinics in hopes of dissuading them from seeking abortions. At times and places secretly scheduled in advance, they stage "rescues," rushing clinic entrances and chaining themselves to the doors to prevent anyone from entering. When police arrive, other volunteers chain themselves to the axles of the police cars to delay the inevitable arrests and bookings that follow these demonstrations.

Women seeking access to the clinics have the general impression that Operation Rescue is there to intimidate and harass them, not to lead them into the light. Pro-choice volunteers gather at abortion clinics in numbers equal to the Rescuers' to reassure patients that they are among supporters and to escort them through the crowds. Arguments and altercations ignite in these almost daily meetings between the two demonstrating factions.

Operation Rescue earned a place in the mainstream, initially, with the warm endorsement of the Roman Catholic church. The *Wanderer*, a conservative Catholic weekly, reported in 1988:

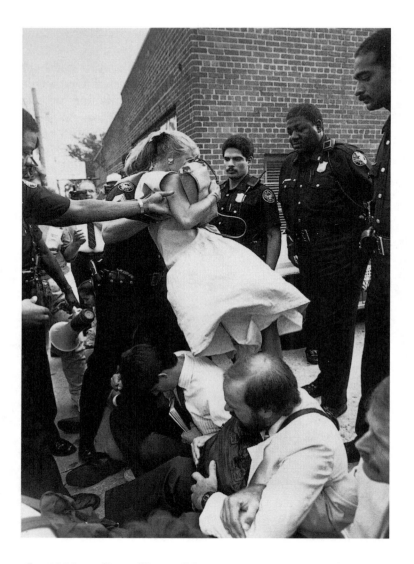

*In 1988, police officers lift a women over antiabortion
protesters blocking the entrance of an Atlanta,
Georgia, abortion clinic. The protesters were members
of Operation Rescue, a group that began blocking the
entrances to abortion clinics in the late 1980s.*

Initial claims by The New York Times *and local television reporters suggested Operation Rescue was the work of the lunatic fringe in the pro-life movement, but this notion was effectively countered when John Cardinal O'Connor agreed to meet May 9th with rescue organizer Randall Terry and three lieutenants. He encouraged them in their work, and granted a photo session with Terry.*[14]

Over the years, OR and groups like it have moved beyond the human blockade that was their hallmark, evolving ingenious and energetic techniques to thwart the work of abortion clinics. Demonstrators have videotaped patients entering and leaving clinics, taken their license plate numbers, threatened clinic employees and prayed out loud for their deaths. The more agile have

"speedbumped"—thrown themselves in front of cars in order to prevent patients and doctors from moving. They ha[ve] "hoodsurfed"— climbed onto patients' cars as they tr[y] to enter clinic parking lots. They ha[ve] driven vans into the front and rear doors of [clinics]. They ha[ve] shackled themselves to cement-filled, rebar-reinforced, fifty-gallon drums at . . . clinic[s]. Some . . . ha[ve] been implicated in arson and butyric acid attacks on abortion clinics. (Butyric acid is an almost ineradicable chemical compound that smells like human vomit.) Some ha[ve] broken into abortion clinics and stolen fetal remains.[15]

Since 1984, the Federal Bureau of Alcohol, Tobacco and Firearms has recorded 149 arson or bomb attacks on abortion clinics.[16]

Investigators sift through rubble at an abortion clinic in Wheaton, Maryland, looking for evidence following a bomb blast.

Despite its hand in all this, OR's reputation for moderation has been secured by the more extreme groups that have come since. The Lambs of Christ, Missionaries to the Preborn, Advocates for Life Ministries, and Army of God—the group responsible for the 1982 kidnapping of an abortion provider and his wife—are just a few of the violent, drifting sects whose methods reinforce the message of the larger and more peaceable pro-life movement. On March 10, 1993, what had been unthinkable first became a reality when Dr. David Gunn, an abortion provider, was shot and killed outside of a clinic in Pensacola Florida. Michael Griffin, the man who murdered him, is a professed Christian who, according to his wife, suffered from "great fits of violence."

Only five months later, Rachelle "Shelley" Shannon, an Oregon housewife, linked with both Army of God and Advocates for Life Ministries, shot Dr. George Tiller, an abortion provider in Wichita, Kansas, in both arms. Shannon was sentenced to serve ten years in prison. Paul Hill, who traveled to Kansas to meet with Shannon the summer after she was incarcerated, became famous on June 29, 1994—the second anniversary of the *Casey* decision—when he shot and killed two people outside a clinic in Pensacola, Florida.

Between the attacks in Kansas and Florida, in November 1994, a sniper armed with an AK-47 assault rifle shot Garson Romalis, an abortion provider in Canada, while he was sitting in his home eating breakfast. Dr. Romalis survived the rupture of his femoral artery. A month later, Don Treshman, leader of the antichoice group Rescue America, said on Canadian radio that the shooting of Dr. Romalis was a "superb tactic" because "the perpetrator got away."[17]

The week after Christmas 1994, John Salvi III, an aspiring hairdresser whom acquaintances described as very religious and a loner, committed a series of attacks that newspapers called a "rampage." First, Salvi pulled a rifle out of a duffel bag and opened fire inside a Planned Parenthood clinic in Brookline, Massachusetts, killing Shannon Lowney, the receptionist, and wounding five others. He then left

Planned Parenthood and went to the Preterm clinic just one mile away. There, he shot Leanne Nichols, the receptionist, and wounded the clinic's armed security guard. The next day, Salvi surfaced in Norfolk, Virginia, where he attempted to force his way into the Hillcrest Clinic, which also performs abortions. Unable to enter, he opened fire on the building before he was finally captured and arrested.

The Roman Catholic church has officially condemned these killings. A recent national poll showed that ninety-seven percent of Americans agree that homicide is not "justifiable" to prevent abortion.[18] Less clear than its stand on murder is the church's stand on arson and vandalism. Mainstream Catholic papers have printed such statements as "destroying property is sometimes a good way to save lives."[19] But even the destruction of property does not appear to satisfy some of the more extreme opponents of abortion. In the wake of every violent act against an abortion provider, the newspapers have quoted apologists explaining that assault and murder will be inevitable until abortion opponents are allowed to protest as vigorously as they want.

On September 8, 1995, Shelley Shannon was brought from the Kansas prison that will be her home until the year 2003 to an Oregon courthouse to face sentencing for her firebomb attacks on women's clinics in California, Nevada, and Oregon. Despite the pleas of her weeping husband and two teenage children, U.S. District Judge James Redden pronounced a sentence of twenty years to start after Shannon has completed her term in Kansas. Judge Redden explained, "Though I am loath to call anyone a terrorist, you are a terrorist."[20]

Leaders of the antiabortion movement rightly fear that the deadly extremes to which activists like Shannon, Salvi, Hill, and Griffin have taken "protest" ultimately damage the credibility of a cause that calls itself "pro-life." Such sensational acts of terrorism also make it easy to forget that earnest and peaceful people come down on both sides of the abortion question. As Luker reminds us:

> *In our society (as in most), the relationship between mother and child is assumed to be the most intimate, most sacred, and most self-sacrificing relationship of all. To people who assume that the embryo is a child, the logic is clear: if even this most sacred, least "worldly," least "useful" relationship can be disrupted, no relationship is safe. As one mother said: "If a baby can't be safe in his mother's womb, where can he be safe?"*[21]

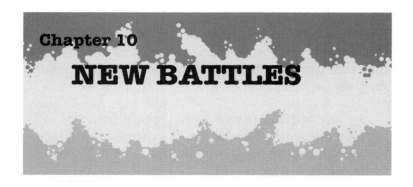

Chapter 10

NEW BATTLES

In 1992, with *Casey*, the Supreme Court seemed finally to have exhausted the topic of abortion and the constitutional right to privacy. The division among the justices was stark and apparent. For almost twenty years, Rehnquist had waited for the fine day when he could write a majority opinion overruling *Roe v. Wade*. But when the *Casey* votes were finally tallied, his side was one short. He wrote an exasperated dissent. Yes, abortion *can* be restricted, he proclaimed. No, it *cannot* be outlawed, he conceded. And there the matter has rested. The nineties have seen parties on both sides of the abortion debate bringing new questions into the courts.

Spurred by the increasingly violent confrontations being staged in front of abortion clinics and doctors' homes, cities around the country have drafted ordinances and courts have issued injunctions to restrain pro-life demonstrators. In recent years, abortion protesters have instituted a series of lawsuits to challenge these regulations, calling on the Supreme Court to specify how much protection the First Amendment affords the "speech" that they carry out in front of America's clinics and in its neighborhoods. It is perhaps ironic that pro-life activists should storm the federal courts claiming they deserve the protection of the same constitutional amendment that guarantees freedom of religion, a liberty they are accused of trampling, but they make no bones about it. Joseph Scheidler, the founder of the Pro-Life Action League, put it this way: "For those who say I can't impose my morality on others, I say just watch me."[1]

The men who wrote the First Amendment understood the power of ideas to incite the kind of mayhem that marks the American abortion debate. They gave us freedom of speech, fully appreciating its potential to stir up trouble. More dangerous than ideas, they believed, is the *fear* of ideas. Years under English tyranny had taught them that the suppression of dissenting views fosters prejudice, not conviction, and that ideas, in any case, cannot be caged. The solution they ordained was free expression and robust debate. They were confident that in the "collision of adverse opinions," the soundest would prevail. The First Amendment, therefore, protects our right to voice and entertain all manner of opinions and to live by the ones that persuade us.

Undergirding our constitutional freedom of expression is the emphatic conviction that "if you can't stand the heat, you should get out of the kitchen." Women seeking abortions cannot be sheltered from bloody images they do not wish to see or harsh words they do not wish to hear. The theory is that a woman who could be dissuaded from ending her pregnancy by a few grisly pictures was perhaps less committed than she realized to her decision to abort. Better she should go home and think it through again.

Though the First Amendment forbids the government to silence ideas, it does not give us absolute freedom of speech. In the interest of order, the government has a well-established right to regulate the time, place, and manner of public demonstrations. And the Supreme Court has always drawn a sharp distinction between conduct and speech—or," sticks and stones" on the one hand, and "names" on the other. The First Amendment protects virtually all forms of speech, however ugly, but it does not protect violence or force, however expressive. It offers no refuge to those who resort to illegal conduct when their words fail to persuade.

Mindful of the established distinction between speech and conduct, Congress passed the Freedom of Access to Clinic Entrances Act of 1994 (FACE), imposing federal penalties on demonstrators who use force or violence to block access to abortion clinics. So far, and not surprisingly, the Supreme Court has declined all invitations to strike down FACE on First Amendment grounds.

Confronted in 1994 with a much closer question, the Court refined a long-standing constitutional distinction between public and private speech. The controversy at the heart of *Madsen v. Women's Health Center, Inc.*[2] arose in Florida, where one physician had already been killed by a pro-life demonstrator. Abortion protesters at the Women's Health Center had violated a series of injunctions—court orders that had been designed to allow them to express their views while preventing them from actually menacing patients as they approached the clinic—when, finally, a Florida judge issued an injunction banning *all* protest activity within thirty feet of the clinic. The protesters sued, claiming that the injunction went much farther than the Constitution allowed.

The protesters had a strong argument. Protecting public speech has always been the core First Amendment value, and courts have been properly hostile to laws that attempt to silence speech in public arenas. They have been more receptive, however, to the regulation of speech that invades private spaces. In public, it is the unwilling listener who must take the trouble to avoid hearing unwelcome speech. At home, in contrast, she has greater rights. She can turn off the radio or ignore the doorbell. When cities have outlawed the focused picketing of a single residence, a favored tactic of pro-life activists, the Supreme Court has upheld their efforts to preserve the privacy of the home.[3] The idea is that a person in her own home, in contrast to a person in a public forum, is a "captive audience." There is nowhere for her to go to escape the message she does not wish to hear.

Although the areas in front of public buildings have traditionally been regarded as classic public spaces, in *Madsen* the Supreme Court suggested that the areas in front of abortion clinics are different. Women who are harassed as they enter clinics, the Court reasoned, are not unlike people trapped in their own homes while demonstrators march outside. Unlike people walking through other public areas who can simply change their route to avoid speech they do not want to hear, patients seeking access to clinics are "held 'captive' by medical circumstance."[4] The Court also noted that the robust debate protected by the First Amendment is not necessarily in harmony with the delivery of health care:

Hospitals . . . are not factories or mines or assembly plants. They are hospitals, where human ailments are treated, where patients and relatives often are under emotional strain and worry, where pleasing and comforting patients are principal facets of the day's activity, and where the patient and his family . . . need a restful, uncluttered, relaxing, and helpful atmosphere.[5]

By this reasoning, the Court has given cities greater latitude to regulate clinic demonstrations than other public speech.

The First Amendment protects our opportunities to persuade and convince others to adopt our way of looking at things. Unfortunately, certain enemies of abortion have discovered that terrorism is vastly more efficient than fair persuasion, and that, if no licensed provider is willing to supply an abortion, there will be no legal abortion.

Unrelenting harassment, vandalism, and threats of harm have driven scores of abortionists to close their doors. At the same time, many of those most stalwart in their commitment to choice, the doctors who served in hospital emergency rooms in the days before *Roe v. Wade*, are reaching retirement age. Of nearly a thousand abortion providers who answered a 1993 survey, two-thirds had "seen a tragedy as a result of an illegal abortion." For the majority of those, it was a motivating factor in their decision to offer abortion services. Of the same group, most are approaching sixty.

New doctors are not eager to become abortionists. Never having witnessed the public health costs of amateur abortion and daunted by the news from "the front," they are taking other career paths. In 1992, only twelve percent of obstetrics and gynecology residency programs provided routine, first trimester abortion training.

Pharmacology holds out the newest hope for an end to the violent confrontations over abortion. RU 486, a compound developed in France in the early eighties, when taken in the first weeks of pregnancy and followed with a prostaglandin (a drug causing uterine contractions), causes a medical miscarriage in ninety-nine out of a hundred cases.[6] Recent studies have shown that methetrexate, a chemotherapy drug that has been on the American market for decades, can be administered with similar results. Since RU 486 became available in France, roughly two million women have used it to terminate their pregnancies with few adverse effects. And, despite the relative ease of taking the drug, the number of women in France who choose to end their pregnancies has not increased.[7]

Neither RU 486 nor methetrexate would completely eliminate the need for surgical abortion. The drugs are effective only in the first weeks of pregnancy, and there will always be women for whom having surgery is medically preferable to taking medication. There is little doubt, however, that the widespread availability of a simple and dependable alternative to surgical abortion would fundamentally transform the debate. Pro-life activists understand better than anyone that it would be infinitely more difficult to target abortionists or women seeking their services if performing an abortion were a simple matter of making a routine examination and writing a prescription, and if ending a pregnancy meant only taking some pills and waiting for a miscarriage.

Although RU 486 has been approved for use in France since 1988, powerful factions in American society succeeded, by lobbying sympathetic politicians, in having the drug banned from the United States until 1992. A dramatic legal challenge to the ban and, more important, the election of a pro-choice president in 1991 have forced the Food and Drug Administration to undertake serious studies of RU 486. And the Population Council, an organization in New York, has been licensed to distribute the drug when and if it is approved. Most medical professionals believe that it is simply a matter of time before the compound will be available in the United States. Dr. David Grimes, the obstetrician-gynecologist who conducted the first American study of RU 486 in the late eighties, says,

French professor Etienne-Emile Beaulieu holds a bottle of RU 486, a pill that can be used to abort a pregnancy.

"the genie is out of the bottle." By this he means that medical knowledge cannot be suppressed any more than religious conviction can be reasoned away or unwanted pregnancy wished away. It remains to be seen whether these advances in science will quiet the public conflict between belief and biology.

Chapter 11
THREE LIVES

HARRY BLACKMUN

In 1994, after serving twenty-five years on the Supreme Court, Harry Blackmun retired at the age of eighty-five. If, as some claim, *Roe* was the most significant thing he did in his long career, it was an achievement that exacted a price. Always prone to overwork—past age eighty, he "could be seen wandering the dark halls of the Court on a Sunday afternoon in search of a working vending machine"[1]—Blackmun also lived most of his years on the High Court under siege. "Once, as antiabortion marchers paraded in front of the Court, he stood watching on the plaza, alone and unnoticed."[2] But hate mail, death threats, and the bullet that screamed into his living room left their mark. Around the Court, he was often peevish and sullen, "a sour little old man," as one clerk described him.[3] In public speeches, he frequently read from the venomous letters that came with every day's mail.

His friends knew a different person—relaxed, charming, and cheerful—when Blackmun was away from his legal work.[4] One remembered watching him and his wife of fifty-three years, Dorothy, together. "They teased each other and had fun like two teenagers,"[5] she said.

To his last days amid the marble and velvet of the

court, Justice Blackmun remained a modest and unassuming man, unshakably devoted to routine. "One egg, toast and coffee every morning at 8 am in the Court cafeteria with his clerks; a four-block walk around the building at lunchtime, [and] a visit to the decrepit exercise room in the Court's basement."[6] Every Saturday night, he sat with his wife in their modest Virginia apartment and listened to "A Prairie Home Companion" on the radio. At a celebration of his eighty-fifth birthday at the Bavarian Beer Garden near Baltimore, he took Dottie out on the dance floor and promised to spend more time with her.

SARAH WEDDINGTON

Sarah Weddington still lives in Austin where since 1981 she has taught pre-law classes on leadership and gender equity at the University of Texas. In the years after *Roe v. Wade* made her famous, Weddington served in Texas as a legislator and in Washington, D.C., as special assistant to President Jimmy Carter. Under Carter, she helped to expand opportunities for women in the military and secured the first funding to help victims of domestic violence. She remains a staunch and ladylike feminist.

Throughout her career, Weddington has traveled the country lecturing about the constitutional right to abortion. She tells stories people have told her:

A woman [in Kansas City, Missouri, received] a call . . . after Clarence Thomas's confirmation from an eighty-two-year-old woman in a nursing home; her physical strength was limited, she said, but she wanted to help save legal abortion and wondered what she could do. . . .

A retired Episcopal priest in a town outside Seattle . . . paid his way through seminary by working at an undertaking establishment. The

*first two bodies he helped with were women
who died after illegal abortions. He is a pro-
choice leader in his community.*

*In Las Vegas, a hotel driver . . . talked
about the pregnancy he and his girlfriend had
chosen to end. They were both working, he was
also in school, and she had a five-year-old
son. They were barely making it. . . . When
they arrived at the clinic, they found an abortion protester had locked himself to the front
door. . . . [H]e wanted to punch the protester
out; his girlfriend prevailed, and they waited
peacefully until the police arrived.*[7]

She tells of being recognized by strangers:

*A few months ago, I was at a rodeo; a vigorous
woman in her forties was going up and down
the aisles selling popcorn. As she came up to
where I was sitting with friends, she stopped
and said, "I know who you are. I'm pro-choice
all the way. Keep up the good work!" . . .*

*The retired woman who ran [the college
guest house in a small town] leaned over to me
while we were watching the news and said,
"Are you the abortion lady?" I didn't know
what was coming next, but I said yes. And she
said, "Well, listen, honey. I watch those men on
TV trying to tell women what to do, and I sit
here and say to them, 'Get your hands off my
body, buster.'"*

*I was standing in an airplane aisle, waiting
to exit, when a man in the opposite aisle . . .
started virtually yelling to me that he couldn't
believe what anti-abortionists were trying to do.
As we were deplaning, a woman caught up
with me and said, "That man told me you*

argued the abortion case. I just want to say thanks for all you've done."[8]

She also tells of receiving hate mail and being checked into hotels under false names to protect her safety.

Sarah's marriage to Ron Weddington ended without bitterness in 1974. He works as a partner in an Austin law firm a few blocks away from his former wife. Of *Roe*, Weddington says, "None of [us] had any idea of the power of what we were unleashing or what we would ultimately accomplish. Even if I had known . . . , I would have gone forward. But it is clear that my life would have been very different if I had said no."

NORMA MCCORVEY

Norma McCorvey lived in peaceful obscurity for sixteen years after *Roe v. Wade*. But in 1989, when the *Webster* case posed the first grave threat to the future of legal abortion, she identified herself as "the real Jane Roe" and began giving interviews. Immediately, McCorvey, who never had an abortion, "became the victim of egg-throwing vandals and the object of [anonymous] hate mail."[10] In April 1990, her living room window, front door, and car window were shattered by shotgun fire. Police believe abortion protesters were responsible. She has come home to find baby clothes scattered across her lawn.

Despite the harassment, she took pride in having played a role in history, calling the Supreme Court decision "my law."[11] But, ironically, abortion rights groups refused to let her speak at a rally outside the Supreme Court in 1989. "She was just some anonymous person who suddenly emerges," explained one pro-choice leader.[12] Gloria Allred, a Los Angeles abortion rights advocate who served as McCorvey's attorney for several years, remembers,

"She was shut out of many national pro-choice cele-
brations. She attended but for the most part she was
not invited and it was a very hurtful experience."[13]

On August 10, 1995, in an interview on ABC's
World News Tonight, McCorvey renounced her belief
in a woman's right to choose abortion, explaining
that she had been haunted by the sight of empty
swings in a playground. "They were swinging back
and forth but they were all empty and I just totally
lost it. And I thought, Oh my God, the playgrounds
are empty because there's not children, because
they've all been aborted."[14]

Soon after she announced her change of heart,
McCorvey refined her views for the press. "I haven't
changed sides all the way," she says. She believes
that abortion should be legal in the first three
months, a view that is fundamentally at odds with
the doctrine of Operation Rescue, the group that
claims credit for her conversion. She explains, "This
is not pro-choice. It is not pro-life. It is pro-Norma."[15]

Activists in the National Right to Life movement
believe McCorvey's "conversion was the ultimate sign
that the staunchest pro-choice advocates, including
women who themselves have had abortions, can and do
change their views."[16] Kate Michelman, the head of the
National Abortion and Reproductive Rights Action
League, took the news in stride. "This movement has
always been about choice, and it's about the right of
every woman to make an individual choice based on her
own individual, religious, moral and ethical beliefs."[17]

Norma still lives in Dallas with Connie
Gonzales. During their years together, they "have
housed a procession of street kids, abused women
and drifters of all types, as well as a succession of
stray cats and dogs."[18]

AFTERWORD

More than any case before or since, *Roe v. Wade* has sparked public debate about the limits of the Supreme Court's authority to say what the Constitution means. Practically speaking, of course, there are no limits. The "court of last resort" has the last word. There is no higher tribunal empowered to review and reverse the Supreme Court's interpretations of the Constitution. There are later courts, staffed by justices who may disagree with the decisions of those who preceded them. But they are expected to recognize the Court as an institution with interests that transcend those of its members. Even when they do not, stare decisis, the principle that the Court must abide by its own prior decisions, checks the justices' power to overrule earlier Court opinions with which they themselves might not agree.

At the same time, for all its authority, the Court has no muscle to enforce its decisions. In the rarest cases, when the Court's word has been met with exceptional resistance, such as some southern states showed to integrating the public schools, the U.S. attorney general has dispatched federal marshals to force compliance. But, as a general matter, credibility is the Supreme Court's only currency.

Decisions that disturb the convictions of a passionate segment of society may provoke intense, and

perhaps unfair, scrutiny, even while those that com-
port with the same group's convictions may be
applauded, regardless of whether they are any more
defensible. The Supreme Court's ruling, for example,
in *Loving v. Virginia*, that there is a constitutional
right to marry, met with little outrage even though
the Constitution makes no mention of marriage. The
same is true of *Griswold v. Connecticut*, the birth control case. No one minds, essentially, that government
has been deprived of the power to say who can marry
or who can have sex without risking pregnancy. In fact,
that a state ever should have had such power seems
faintly absurd.

Most everyone agrees that the Constitution pro-
tects more rights than it names. The Ninth
Amendment plainly says so: "The enumeration in the
Constitution of certain rights shall not be construed
to deny or disparage others retained by the people."
There is also little dispute that it is for the Supreme
Court to say what those "other" rights are, and—
because legislatures are free to regulate any activity
that is *not* protected by the Constitution—that the
Court should say what they are. Yet, the Supreme
Court is never more at the mercy of public opinion
than when it announces the existence of a right the
Constitution does not specifically mention.

The Court's credibility is on the line any time it can
be accused of having stepped off the page and pulled a
constitutional right out of thin air. Mindful of its vul-
nerability, the Court has tried to find a dispassionate
approach to naming the unenumerated rights the Constitution protects. In 1937, Justice Benjamin Cardozo
wrote that any interest that was "so rooted in the tradi-
tions and conscience of our people as to be ranked as
fundamental" was worthy of constitutional protection
under the due process clause's promise of liberty.[1]

What facets of our "liberty" are "fundamental"?

Cardozo proposed this test to tell the answer: could one imagine a civilized society in which a legislature was free to regulate this particular activity? If not, then the activity was fundamental—worthy of constitutional protection and untouchable. More recently, the Court has said that constitutional liberty interests must be not only "fundamental" but "traditionally protected by our society."[2] Finding them requires "respect for the teachings of history [and] solid recognition of the basic values that underlie our society." In a very real sense, this is how the Court tries to write our deepest intuitions into law.

The trouble, some argue, is that the Supreme Court doesn't *know* "our society." The United States is home to infinitely more kinds of people than have ever sat on the High Court, as the most cursory history shows. There had never been an African-American appointed to the Court until 1967, when Thurgood Marshall was picked. And it was 1981 before the first woman, Sandra Day O'Connor, made the roster. Some claim that when the Supreme Court seeks the "basic values that underlie our society," it naturally finds the values of its own members.

When Norma McCorvey asked Connie Gonzales, "How would you like to meet Jane Roe?" Connie laughed because, as she put it, "Come on, we don't know anybody like that." Although Connie did in fact know someone very much like Jane Roe, her insight was true. She meant, "people who make the front page of the *Dallas Times-Herald* bringing famous cases to the Supreme Court are heterosexual, solvent, and educated; we're not. The Supreme Court does not trouble itself with people like us."

Some have argued that the fate of *Roe v. Wade* proves Connie's point. They remind us that women like Sarah Weddington, with years of schooling and $400, managed to get safe abortions even in pre-*Roe*

Texas, while women like Norma McCorvey, poor and ignorant, did not. For poor women, they point out, little has changed: the funding prohibitions the Court first upheld in 1980 make abortions as unobtainable as criminal prohibitions made them before 1973. They argue that the Supreme Court's indifference to circumstances like poverty reflects this reality: the members of the Supreme Court know the Sarah Weddingtons of the world but it does not know the Norma McCorveys.

Supreme Court justices are not supposed to let their personal opinions infect their judicial opinions. In *Griswold*, the Connecticut birth control case, Justice Hugo Black made this point in gruff dissent:

> *I get nowhere in this case by talk about a constitutional 'right of privacy' [derived] from one or more constitutional provisions. I like my privacy as well as the next one, but I am nevertheless compelled to admit that government has a right to invade it unless prohibited by some specific constitutional provision.*[3]

Although a majority of Black's colleagues readily found privacy in the Constitution, many of them have had a difficult time envisioning a right spacious enough to protect activities they cannot imagine wishing to pursue. As one constitutional scholar has written, "The boundaries of the right to privacy turned out to be the sensibilities of the ruling class."[4]

The Constitution is for everyone—the rich, the poor, the unconventional, and the mainstream. In the abstract, most of our rights sound innocuous, even wholesome. But, understand that the freedom of religion includes the freedom to be an atheist, to worship the devil, or to practice a faith that requires the ritual sacrifice of animals.[5] The right to free speech embraces

erotic dancing as well as fomenting racial hatred.[6]
The right to marry allows us to marry brutal crimi-
nals. The right to bring up children includes the privi-
lege to raise them in squalor and ignorance. And the
right to make one's own reproductive decisions
includes the rights to have an abortion, to have one
baby or many. *Roe v. Wade* protects a woman from
forced abortion just as it protects her from forced
childbearing. Constitutionally speaking, these are
interests that go hand in hand. And, although we may
find some of them distasteful or even shocking, most
of us would not consider doing without the rights that
protect them. If, in some future America overcrowded
and underfed, a legislature tried to curb the population by passing a law that prevented women from
having more than one child, a woman who was pregnant for the second time could sue to invalidate the
law. *Roe v. Wade* is a case she would cite.

Every unwanted pregnancy poses a dilemma that
roughly half the population has the biological luxury
never to face. To the men who have always dominated
our courts and legislatures, lobbied by the fervent
Christians who have recently dominated the news,
abortion may appear to be a dispensable option. But
for many women, it is an option that makes a world
of difference.

The gulf of experience that separates the sexes on
this issue was never more starkly revealed than in
the bitter fight that followed Clarence Thomas's nomination to the Supreme Court. Judge Thomas's qualifi-
cations were widely debated, his character was called
into question by allegations of sexual harassment,
and he would not reveal his views on abortion. A
parade of prominent women took the stand to testify
against his appointment before the Senate Judiciary
Committee. Madeleine Kunin, the former governor of
Vermont, spoke most eloquently:

The very fact that Judge Thomas has succeeded in not clarifying his philosophy on this issue creates a quiet fury in many women. Once again, when it comes to our issues, we find ourselves repeating the ancient cycle of helplessness that women have experienced throughout history. The sense of powerlessness is painful. It is apparent right here in this room, where women are not equally represented in the decision-making process of this country. . . . We are put in the position of pleaders, asking you to ask our questions for us, to be our stand-ins, to intercede on our behalf. Once again, our question, central to our lives, the one that women all over this country are asking, is not being answered. We have to take our chances. We have to live on hope. We have to believe that silence equals fairness when, in fact, we fear that silence equals just the opposite."[7]

The Senate confirmed Kunin's fears, and Thomas's appointment, by a narrow margin.

Abortion is not unconventional. It is the most common surgical procedure American women undergo, at a rate of 1.6 million every year. One-fifth of American women over the age of fifteen have had an abortion. Most are young and single. More than one-fourth are teenagers. More than two-thirds say they could not afford the child or felt otherwise unready for motherhood.[8]

For priests and politicians to treat abortion as a new and justly controversial issue is to rewrite theological and American history. Justice Stevens pointed out in his dissent from the *Webster* case that the official position of the Roman Catholic church "from the church's very conception up until Pope Pius IX's 1869 decree held that the fetus did not become a person until late in the course of gestation."[9] The people who settled our shores likewise treated abortion "with benign toleration. From the 1660s through 1776, the colonies, following English common law, permitted abortion everywhere. The Constitution contain[s] no mention of abortion because, most scholars agree, the practice was widely accepted."[10]

Despite our history of tolerance and despite current polls consistently showing that most Americans believe the abortion choice belongs to the pregnant woman, abortion opponents—numerically a minority—doggedly try to make life miserable for seekers, providers, and supporters of legal abortion. In these times, abortion has become a litmus test for politicians. Legislators make careers by saying how much they would like to get their hands on abortion rights, if only the Supreme Court would overrule *Roe v. Wade*. But before *Roe*, they were saying something entirely different. Bob Packwood, the lately disgraced senator from Oregon, said in 1971, "Most of the legislators in the nation I have met and many members of Congress would prefer the Supreme Court to legalize abortion, thereby taking them off the hook and relieving them of the responsibility for decision-making."[11]

Roe v. Wade was meant to place abortion with other private choices above the tumult of politics. There will always be fighting about abortion. And there will always be abortion. But if career-minded legislators persist in flouting the spirit of *Roe*, and pro-life activists persist in lawless violence, the day may come when legal abortion in America is history. It is a day we have already seen.

SOURCE NOTES

CHAPTER ONE

1. Blackmun with Bill Moyers, "In Search of the Constitution: Mr. Justice Blackmun," 26 April 1987, PBS.
2. David Savage, *Turning Right, The Making of the Rehnquist Supreme Court* (New York: Wiley, 1992), 233.
3. David Garrow, *Liberty and Sexuality: The Right to Privacy and the Making of Roe v. Wade* (New York: Macmillan, 1994), 474.
4. Margaret Carlson, "Old Number Three Goes Home," *Time*, April 18, 1994, 36.
5. Savage, 237.
6. Ibid., 234.
7. Sarah Weddington, *A Question of Choice* (New York: Putnam, 1992), 17.
8. Ibid., 19.
9. Ibid., 261.
10. Ibid.
11. Ibid., 14.
12. Ibid.
13. Norma McCorvey with Andy Meisler, *I Am Roe* (New York: HarperCollins, 1994), 14.
14. Ibid., 15.
15. Ibid.
16. Michelle Green, "The Woman Behind *Roe v. Wade,*" *People Weekly*, May 22, 1989, 36.
17. McCorvey, 77.
18. Ibid., 101.
19. Ibid., 105.

CHAPTER TWO

1. Garrow, 393.
2. Savage, 45.
3. Weddington, 25.
4. Ibid., 26.
5. Garrow, 390.
6. Ibid.
7. Laurence Tribe, *Abortion: The Clash of Absolutes* (New York: Norton, 1992), 41, citing James Mohr, *Abortion in America: The Origins and Evolution of National Policy, 1800–1900* (New York: Oxford Univ. Press, 1978), 254.
8. Weddington, 40.
9. Ibid., 34.
10. Ibid., 43.
11. Ibid., 27.
12. Garrow, 391.
13. Ibid., 392.
14. Tribe, 40.
15. Weddington, 32.
16. Ibid., 33.
17. Ibid., 37.
18. Ibid., 35.
19. Ibid., 39.
20. Tribe, 29.
21. Garrow, 395.
22. Ibid.
23. Allen v. Wright, 468 U.S. 737, 751 (1984).
24. Garrow, 400.

CHAPTER THREE

1. McCorvey, 104.
2. Ibid.
3. Ibid., 106.
4. Ibid., 112.
5. Ibid.
6. Ibid., 113.
7. Ibid.
8. Ibid.
9. Ibid., 117.
10. Ibid., 118.

11. Ibid., 119.
12. Ibid., 119.
13. Ibid., 118–19.
14. Ibid., 119–20.
15. Ibid., 120.
16. Ibid., 121.
17. Ibid., 121–22.
18. Ibid., 122.
19. Weddington, 60.
20. Weddington, 56.
21. Garrow, 406.
22. Ibid., 56.
23. Garrow, 436.
24. Weddington, 56.
25. Garrow, 436.

CHAPTER FOUR
1. See *Barnes v. Glen Theatres, Inc.*, 501 U.S. 560 (1991).
2. Tribe, 107 (citing Powell, "The Original Understanding of Original Intent," *Harvard Law Review* 98 (1985), 885, 936, quoting *Letters and Other Writings of James Madison* 3 (1865), 53, 54, 228).
3. Excerpt from Brief for the State, *Muller v. Oregon*, 208 U.S. 412 (1908).
4. Woodrow Wilson, *Constitutional Government in the United States* (1908), 192, quoted in Michael Kammen, *Sovereignty and Liberty* (Madison: Univ. of Wisconsin Press, 1988), 141.
5. See *Loving v. Virginia*, 388 U.S. 1 (1967).
6. 262 U.S. 390 (1923).
7. Tribe, 92.
8. *Meyer*, 262 U.S. at 399.
9. 268 U.S. 510 (1925).
10. *Pierce*, 268 U.S. at 534–35.
11. Tribe, 92–93, quoting Pierce, 268 U.S. at 535; Meyer, 262 U.S. at 402.
12. Tribe, 93.
13. *Skinner v. Oklahoma*, 316 U.S. 535, 536 (1942).
14. Ibid. at 541.
15. 381 U.S. 479 (1965).

CHAPTER FIVE
1. Tribe, 37.
2. Kristin Luker, *Abortion and the Politics of Motherhood* (Berkeley: Univ. of California Press, 1984), 64.
3. Ibid.
4. Garrow, 287.
5. Luker, 64.
6. Garrow, 289.
7. Ibid.
8. Luker, 87.
9. Ibid., 88.
10. Weddington, 76.
11. Garrow, 430.
12. Weddington, 76.
13. Garrow, 279–80.
14. Weddington, 79.
15. Tribe, 40, quoting Lawrence Lader, *Abortion II* (Boston: Beacon, 1973), 30.
16. Tribe, 39.
17. Ibid., 41.
18. Garrow, 483.
19. Tribe, 50.
20. Garrow, 578.
21. Garrow, 563.
22. Garrow, 577.
23. Tribe, 50, citing Leismer, "Abortion Reform—Election's Most Emotional Issue," *Detroit News*, November 6, 1972, 3A.
24. Tribe, 50, citing Leismer.
25. Garrow, 578.
26. Garrow, 482, 483.
27. Tribe, 51.
28. Kathleen M. Sullivan, *"Liberty and Sexuality: The Right to Privacy and the Making of Roe v. Wade* (Book Review)," *New Republic*, May 23, 1994, describing how Garrow accounts for the failure of efforts to reform or repeal abortion laws.
29. Garrow, 579.

CHAPTER SIX
1. Garrow, 396–97.
2. Ibid., 434; Weddington, 59.

3. Garrow, 435–36 (internal quotation omitted).
4. Ibid., 441–42.
5. Ibid., 443.
6. Ibid.
7. Ibid., 453–54; Weddington, 67–68.
8. Garrow, 454; Weddington, 70.
9. Weddington, 70.
10. Garrow, 454–55.
11. Savage, 52; Weddington, 72.
12. McCorvey, 124–25.
13. Ibid., 126.
14. Ibid.
15. Ibid., 126–27.
16. Ibid., 131.

CHAPTER SEVEN
1. Weddington, 81.
2. Ibid., 83.
3. Garrow, 514–15 (citing Lucas [letter] to Weddington, 7 November 1971, Lucas Box 7).
4. McCorvey, 146.
5. Ibid.
6. Garrow, 516.
7. Ibid., 517.
8. Weddington, 107.
9. Peter Irons and Stephanie Guitton, eds., *May It Please the Court* (New York: New Press, 1993), 344–45.
10. Ibid, 345.
11. Ibid.
12. Ibid.
13. Ibid., 346.
14. Ibid.
15. Ibid.
16. Ibid.
17. Garrow, 526, citing Margie Hames's account of the argument.
18. Irons and Guitton, 347.
19. Ibid.
20. Ibid., 348.
21. Ibid.

22. Weddington, 120.
23. Irons and Guitton, 348.
24. Garrow, 563–64.
25. Weddington, 134–35.
26. Garrow, 565.
27. Weddington, 136.
28. Irons and Guitton, 349.
29. Ibid., 350.
30. Weddington, 138.
31. Garrow, 569.
32. Weddington, 139.
33. Ibid.
34. Irons and Guitton, 351.
35. Garrow, 569.
36. Ibid.
37. Weddington, 140.
38. Irons and Guitton, 351.
39. Ibid., 352; Weddington, 141.
40. Weddington, 141.
41. Ibid.
42. Irons and Guitton, 353.
43. Ibid.

CHAPTER EIGHT
1. Weddington, 145.
2. Ibid., 146.
3. 410 U.S. 113, 116 (1973).
4. 410 U.S. at 125.
5. Weddington, 170.
6. 410 U.S. at 129–30.
7. 410 U.S. at 152–53.
8. 410 U.S. at 153.
9. 410 U.S. at 159–60.
10. 410 U.S. at 162.
11. 410 U.S. at 210, Douglas, J., concurring.
12. 410 U.S. at 213, Douglas, J., concurring [quoting *Eisenstadt v. Baird*, 405 U.S. 438, 453 (1972)].
13. 410 U.S. at 214–15, Douglas, J., concurring.
14. 410 U.S. 221–22, White, J., dissenting.
15. McCorvey, 143.
16. Ibid., 145.

17. Ibid., 148.
18. Ibid.

CHAPTER NINE
1. Luker, 137–38.
2. Ibid., 141.
3. Ibid., 137.
4. Ibid., 197.
5. 448 U.S. 297 (1980).
6. The Alan Guttmacher Institute.
7. 492 U.S. 490 (1989).
8. 497 U.S. 417 (1990).
9. Savage, 344.
10. Ibid.
11. 500 U.S. 173 (1991).
12. Weddington, 111.
13. Randall Terry, Executive Director, Operation Rescue, and the Reverend Daniel J. Little in Terry's film, *Higher Laws*, video produced by Project Life, © March 1987; distributed by American Portrait Films.
14. Paul Likoudis, "Operation Rescue a Success," *Wanderer*, May 19, 1988.
15. Verlyn Klinkenborg, "Violent Certainties," *Harper's Magazine*, January 1995, 40.
16. Ana Puga, "Newcomers Preach Violence," *Boston Sunday Globe*, October 30, 1994.
17. "A Time to Kill," "The 5th Estate," Canadian Broadcasting Company, December 13, 1994. Julian Sher, producer; Howard Goldenthal, associate producer.
18. Time/CNN poll cited in Planned Parenthood Alameda/San Francisco Newsletter, Spring 1995, 1.
19. Mary Meehan, Anti-Choice Columnist, *National Catholic Register*, January 4, 1987.
20. "Woman Gets 20 Years in Abortion Clinic Attacks," *New York Times*, September 9, 1995.
21. Luker, 156.

CHAPTER TEN
1. Joseph Scheidler, Executive Director, Pro-Life Action League, *Pro-Life Action News*, August 8, 1989.

2. 114 S. Ct. 2516 (1994).
3. See *Frisby v. Schultz*, 487 U.S. 474 (1987).
4. *Madsen*, 114 S. Ct. at 2526
5. *Madsen* at 2528 [quoting *NLRB v. Baptist Hospital, Inc.*, 442 U.S. 773, 783–84 (1978) (Blackmun, J., concurring opinion)].
6. *New England Journal of Medicine*, May 1993.
7. *Wall Street Journal*, February 22, 1993.

CHAPTER ELEVEN
1. Savage, 236.
2. Ibid.
3. Savage, 237.
4. Savage, 238.
5. Ibid.
6. Margaret Carlson, "Old Number Three Goes Home," *Time*, April 18, 1994, v. 143, n. 16, p. 36.
7. Weddington, 264–66.
8. Ibid., 265.
9. Ibid., 261.
10. Michelle Green, "The Woman Behind *Roe v. Wade*," *People Weekly*, May 22, 1989, 36.
11. Ibid.
12. Steven Waldman and Ginny Carroll, "*Roe v. Roe*," *Newsweek*, August 21, 1995, p.22.
13. Sam Howe Verhovek, "New Twist for a Landmark Case: *Roe v. Wade* Become *Roe v. Roe*," *New York Times*, August 12, 1995, p. 1.
14. Ibid.
15. Waldman and Carroll.
16. Ibid.
17. Washington Reuters, August 11, 1995.
18. Michelle Green, "The Woman Behind *Roe v. Wade*," *People Weekly*, May 22, 1989, v. 31, n. 20, p. 36.

AFTERWORD
1. *Palko v. Connecticut*, 302 U.S. 319, 325 (1937).
2. *Michael H. v. Gerald D.*, 491 U.S. 110, 122–23 (1989) (citations omitted).

3. *Griswold v. Connecticut*, 381 U.S. at 509–10 (Black, J., dissenting).
4. Sullivan.
5. See *Church of the Lukumi Babalu Aye, Inc. v. City of Hialeah*, 113 S. Ct. 2217 (1994).
6. See *R.A.V. v. City of St. Paul*, Minnesota, 503 U.S. 377 (1992).
7. Weddington, 231.
8. Richard Lacayo, "Whose Life Is It?" *Time*, May 1, 1989, v. 133, n. 18, p. 20, citing statistics from the Alan Guttmacher Institute.
9. Stephen T. Asma, "Abortion and the Embarrassing Saint," *The Humanist*, May-June 1994 v. 54, n. 3, p. 30.
10. Roger Rosenblatt, "Welcome to Uncomfortable Times," *U.S. News & World Report*, July 17, 1989, v. 107, n. 3, p. 8.
11. Garrow, 482.

FURTHER READING AND VIEWING

Bennetts, Leslie. "A Woman's Choice." *Vanity Fair*, September 1992.

Bonavoglia, Angela, ed. *The Choices We Made: 25 Women and Men Speak Out About Abortion*. New York: Random House, 1991.

Caruana, Claudia. *The Abortion Debate*. Brookfield, CT: Millbrook Press, 1992.

Costa, Maria. *Abortion: A Reference Handbook*. Santa Barbara: ABC-CLIO, 1991.

Cozic, Charles P., and Stacey Tipp, eds. *Abortion: Opposing Viewpoints*. San Diego: Greenhaven, 1991.

Emmens, Carol. *The Abortion Controversy*. New York: Julian Messner, 1987.

Faux, Marian. *Roe v. Wade: The Untold Story of the Landmark Supreme Court Decision That Made Abortion Legal*. New York: Macmillan, 1988.

Flanders, Carl N. *Abortion*. New York: Facts On File, 1990.

Garrow, David. *Liberty and Sexuality: The Right to Privacy and the Making of* Roe v. Wade. New York: Macmillan, 1994.

Irons, Peter, and Stephanie Guitton, eds. *May It Please the Court.* New York: New Press, 1993.

Luker, Kristin. *Abortion and the Politics of Motherhood.* Berkeley: Univ. of California Press, 1984.

McCorvey, Norma, with Andy Meisler, *I Am Roe.* New York: HarperCollins, 1994.

"Roe v. Wade." A made-for-television movie based on the case; first broadcast by NBC in 1989.

Rubin, Eva R., ed. *The Abortion Controversy: A Documentary History.* Westport, CT: Greenwood, 1994.

Terkel, Susan N. *Abortion: Facing the Issues.* New York: Franklin Watts, 1988.

Tribe, Laurence H. *Abortion: The Clash of Absolutes.* New York: Norton, 1992.

Weddington, Sarah. *A Question of Choice.* New York: Putnam, 1992.

INDEX